The University of Life

A Journey of the Mind

STEVEN PRICE

Copyright © 2024 Steven Price

All rights reserved.

ISBN-13: 979-8-3436-6629-8

DEDICATION

I dedicate this book, the first volume of the UoL series, to my late Great Uncle Frank. His knowledge and wisdom assisted me in finding literature that helped enable me to describe experiences not so easily described. He made me aware of great philosophers and writers of our past, such as Carl Jung and Abraham Maslow from the west and Maharishi Mahesh Yogi from the east; all who have explained the finer states of being. I am eternally grateful to Frank and Maharishi for bringing me into contact with my own Being, through the practice of Transcendental Meditation.

CONTENTS

	Acknowledgement	i
	Authors Note	iii
	Prologue	v
	PART 1 – FRACTURING OF THE MIND	1
1	Where it all starts	1
2	Drug induction	5
3	In training	11
4	The old smoke	18
5	Chester races	31
6	Barbados and the West Indies	45
7	Black magic	67
8	Shiatsu	72
9	Ghost writing	74
10	Three little birds	79
11	Voices	83
12	Departure	87
13	Arrival	91
	PART 2 – PSYCHIATRIC MONOPOLY	99
14	Breakout of Basingstoke I	99
15	Dual of the carriageway	101
16	Meeting the wizard	103
17	The infamous blue blanket	107
18	The dice & the chair leg	111
19	Breakout of Basingstoke	114
20	Follow the moon to Newbury	118
21	Kings Cross, St Pancreas	122
22	A Stop at Stirling	125
23	Risk assessment	127

24	Falkirk, Ward 19 Psychiatric Unit	129
25	Cold turkey	132
26	Everything is everything	135
27	Radio oneness	139
28	Pink rabbits n' ice	142
29	Stirling and the freemasons	151
30	Femininity vs masculinity	162
31	Back to reality	166
	PART 3 – REHABILITATION	168
32	Chi Gong	168
33	Loch Katrine	171
34	Change your mind	175
35	Bhagavad Gita	185
36	Relapse	193
37	AA	196
38	Yoga & the meaning of life	202
39	Conscious cycles	206
40	Real life risk assessment	208
41	Cutting out the caffeine	213
42	Back to the future	215
43	Transcendental deep meditation	218
44	Right thinking left feeling	224
45	Peace & tranquil-i-tea	231

ACKNOWLEDGMENTS

Thank you for everyone involved in my recovery, from the NHS doctors and nurses, to my family, with special thanks to my Auntie and Uncle who looked after me and got me back on my feet following release from the mental hospital.

Thank you to all the sources mentioned within this book, your knowledge has helped me understand myself, my addictions and enabled me to maintain a healthy recovery.

Thank you to my lovely creative wife to be, for everything you do for me and a big thanks for your amazing artwork of the rising Phoenix, that forms the cover of this book.

Thank you to my Mum, Dad and my Sisters, who have always stood by me, and never judged.

Finally, thank you to my amazing daughters, who by just being there, helped me maintain a healthy existence.

STEVEN PRICE

AUTHORS NOTE

Greetings brothers and sisters of the planet earth, we are gathered here today to unite in what appears to be a very unsettled world full of despair and hopeless reasoning. This story is a factual reflection on life, its crazy encounters and influences and most importantly the over comings of these.

Alcoholism, drug abuse, mental disorders, a trip to three psychiatric hospitals and rehabilitation are all covered, including some handy tips on controlling one's addictions and emotions. Of course, the primary objective is to lead you readers with problems or not, down an easier path; avoiding all or at least some of the aforementioned disaster areas!

The book focuses on one young man of the name Steve-O, no not the crazy Steve-O from Jackass, the other crazy ass Steve-O from Scotland.

Yes, that's me.

Join me on an exciting madcap adventure from the four corners of the UK to the West Indies island of Barbados, including a harrowing sailing journey to the island of Bequia in the Grenadines. Witness the subtle links between everyday reality and madness. Come to understand the mechanics of our minds that cause mental illness, without the pain of enduring a psychosis.

The journey to insanity and back again begins with sharing the experiences of drug abuse. Be warned that some of the material including the explicit drug taking stories, may entice some of you to try drugs and if you are already on the brink of doing so, I ask that you finish the book before taking that step to insanity. The reasoning for not taking drugs is covered within and entails a horrific ordeal of "cold turkey", which should be enough to put anyone off the idea of trying them in the first instance.

For those of us already in the mire, getting out is a slippery and tricky affair. If followed to the end, this story shall effortlessly provide the tools required for self-awareness, because the mind is naturally inquisitive about it's own nature and will enjoy the journey to the depths within.

STEVEN PRICE

THE UNIVERSITY OF LIFE; A JOURNEY OF THE MIND

PROLOGUE

As mind and body work together to hold on to reality via duality, words are formed that are equal and opposite to the thoughts as they occur. Mind and body run out of ways to remind the self of life, which is a series of continual duality; the ego disappears after intense fear of losing oneself and then there is the void. The place where no thoughts or action are possible, the place that you cannot describe because its nature is infinite, unlimited and unbounded. Whereas life is bound by cause and effect and has limits of opposing natures.

The main failure people make in trying to understand the phenomena of madness is to label it as I have just done! It can only be hinted towards by the finest thought, to experience it is entirely different and to imagine it is impossible. The re-occurring fear of being close to the question of life, the question that is so unique, simple, and of the finest earliest thought possible, is that the answer is the question.

This is a very dangerous position to find oneself in, because it can come naturally and the more you try not to think about it the more it can present itself. For people with obsessive natures the need to know surpasses the fear of feeling that it is dangerous.

The subconscious takes over and the thoughts come naturally, when they can't connect with reasonable answers the thoughts begin to come faster, racing thoughts give way to manic thinking, and eventually mania takes over.

Reality within insanity is a thoughtless void, of potential vastness where although you don't recognise where you are, you have an awareness of being interconnected to everything.

It is absolute.

You are the tree, the wind blowing the leaves, the energy being you would think you are (if you could think) and yet you have no place to go, because you are everywhere, so how do you get out?

Are you scared?

What is your fear?

That you can't get back to yourself, your lost identity and ego?

Exactly, it is not that you are anxious there, it is the process of falling into the void and getting out that is scary. For it is at these tipping over the edge moments that you are aware of both yourself and the lingering vastness of potential. It is a dangerous game.

The only safe way to experience the unbounded awareness is via safe slow meditation practise. You may come out of meditation and realise that you were gone a while, but you are at a restful state of alertness and therefore at peace.

There is no anxiety, or fear of losing your identity, it is a natural process of Self realisation: of releasing stress and experiencing 200% of life as Maharishi Mahesh Yogi would say. 100% physical (bounded) and 100% spiritual (unbounded), at the same time.

For anyone seeking answers to the unknown, the occult world; and trying to mentally fathom ones existence, I say:

Stop thinking.

PART 1 - FRACTURING OF THE MIND

1 WHERE IT ALL STARTS

For many it all starts and ends in the hospital, for me it all began in Scotland. Born in 1979, a healthy drug and alcohol-free baby or so my delighted parents thought. Alcoholism begins for most of our population at a very, very young age, as the influential demon is already present as a hereditary nuisance.

Although not all alcoholics or troubled drinkers can claim hereditary problems, for most people the DNA cells are poisoned from birth.

From the moment you pop out at birth and say hello to your adoring parents you may well already be harbouring the most dangerous, addictive and widespread disease that plagues our population world-wide.

The main problem affecting us alcoholics, we want to drink our pint or long vodka or glass of wine like it is the last one we'll ever see. There is a reason behind this fast-drinking habit that causes far too many of us problems, such as having no money for one! Ever been in a situation where all the drinkers around you are still sipping on theirs and you are almost finished and eyeballing the bar?

Personally, I spent a fortune in my boozing days buying rounds in between rounds. When you buy someone a drink before their round's up, it's not very often you get reimbursed and yes, people do notice that you're edgy for another drink. This would be fine if it was just a one off.

Often this is where it all starts to go downhill. At this stage, you no doubt will be a keen pub activist claiming you like watching football and other sports, when really you just need an excuse to be down the pub on your own. Or you regularly sup a bottle of wine at the end of your shift, whilst your partner is still at work, or oddly enough in the pub after a stressful day in the office.

Oh don't ask about the bar staff!

"Honest, I never even paid them a glance, read the paper is all."

Recently I read an article in a newspaper concerning the death of a young career woman due to excessive daily drinking brought on by stress. A lady that has managed to help others escape this misfortune wrote a book called 'Sober and Staying that Way'. Her name is Susan Powter and I came across her book during a rare moment of realisation of my excessive drinking back in the early 2000's.

So getting back to the reason behind fast alcohol consumption: according to Susan, it has an awful lot to do with the hereditary issue, the liver, and the brain. The full title of her book includes 'The Missing Link in the Cure for Alcoholism' and it was this knowledge that the majority of people suffering from alcoholism contain a different metabolism in their liver regarding the chemical acetaldehyde than that of a non-alcoholic person; that enabled me to begin to understand that we are not mentally capable of abstinence without physical assistance.

Acetaldehyde, phonetically spelt Ass-a-tol-da-hyde, is a pain in the ass hyde! It is the poison that makes us high.

Alcoholism IS a progressive disease, physically as well as psychologically. The physical aspects we hear people talk of can be explained at a high level, in not too complicated a way.

The liver turns alcohol into acetaldehyde and then into acetate, then it can be removed from the body when we go for a pee; hopefully not on the couch at five in the morning!

In a normal liver the alcohol turns into acetaldehyde and then into acetate at a rate relative to the consumption and if overindulgence occurs then the person will generally feel sick and stop drinking.

You all know those people who have their drinking under control; they make you sick don't they? Well here's the reason.

Now presume you have hereditary alcoholism, what happens is the alcohol in your liver turns into acetaldehyde far quicker than that of a person with a normal liver metabolism. To add to this problem the process of turning acetaldehyde in your liver to acetate is slower than that of a normal liver.

Therefore, the liver then floods with the poison acetaldehyde and this in turn infects your brain through the blood system creating a real high effect and inducing confidence. Hence drink drivers think they can take the sharpest corners at high speeds and get away with it, their high of course!

Additionally, this process of poisoning the brain creates an addictive tendency in that the consumer wants more alcohol to remain high and even increase it. Though legal in most countries it is one of the most dangerous drugs in my opinion, due to its progressive nature and also due to the behaviour of the consumer that it causes.

It may not kill you immediately, although we all know that the effects of it can. However, if taken repetitively for some time, the poison will eventually take over your body. In due course your inner organs will become so infected that even a transplant may not save you, even if you can get one.

Unfortunately, we're not all as lucky as good ole George Best;

"Pint of your best bitter please mate".

A famous Manchester United footballer who obtained a liver transplant on the NHS, only to be seen drinking again sometime afterwards, which as you can imagine was highly controversial given his obvious alcoholism.

Accept it boys and girls, you're doomed by your genes to be an alcoholic, there is no in-between. Knowing these facts can help a person with alcoholic tendencies to gain control and maintain recovery. For people who have to deal with alcoholic loved ones, knowing that they are being controlled and not themselves, this knowledge is also helpful.

Anyone in my opinion with alcoholism can gain control but it takes a holistic approach and continual awareness.

From experience I believe it is possible to control the consumption and the effects, however the work involved is sometimes not worth the hassle, trust me it is easier to abstain, and far more rewarding eventually.

2 DRUG INDUCTION

Life as a boy growing up in a fairly remote part of Scotland was amazing, a very happy childhood with lots of things to do, being the outdoor kind of guy that I was and still am. I have very fond memories of my early childhood.

Our old house was around 150 years old and was the Lodge to a very big house next door. The big house was split into three flats and was just at the top of the drive. On the other side of the lodge was another drive leading up to two large properties. Beyond this the nearest property was a farm in one direction and the main village was about half a mile away in the other direction.

The lodge where we lived had a small stream running down from the hillside and this flowed past the house under a bridge to our front door and then under another bridge in the front garden. The main road was directly in front of the house and the burn ran under the road through a tunnel that an adult could walk under if they bent their head.

When the burn was not racing too fast you could walk through the tunnel to the pebbly beach with boots on. It was a great move from a larger town nearby around the age of six. Being quite a large town it had a reputation for youth crime and drugs and so my parents thought it would be better bringing me up somewhere out the way of trouble.

The lodge had an open fire in the snug that heated the water. Coal and logs fuelled the fire and this required a regular stock of kindling and firewood that had to be cut in the back garden.

My Dad made me my first axe when I was about seven or eight years old and in the years to come I would do a lot of the chopping myself, together with collecting two to three buckets of coal a day from the bunker in the front garden. This provided good character building and was hard work but the best part for me as a youngster was the fishing.

My first ever time catching a fish for myself was with my cousin. We hooked this jack Pike on a small spinner. Pike, even baby jack ones are renowned for their dangerous bite as their teeth interlock and grow backwards. One bite of the finger and that's it – Gone!

So we catch this fish, not knowing what it was and I carry it alive all the way up the hill to our caravan, which is situated in the grounds of a bed and breakfast.

My Mum, not knowing what it was took us down to the B&B house to where this old man who owned the place was feeding his chickens. When he realised that this Pike was still alive he quickly took it off us and killed it, we were completely in awe when he showed us the teeth.

It is important to recognise that problems can arise from a normal upbringing and therefore illustrate a very real-life experience that can be compared to the average person.

Actually I dislike the word 'normal', because it's a relative term depending upon who's using it. However, hopefully you know what I mean.

All my memories of my younger childhood are bright and I think this is due to the fact that our family was happy.

However, there was some boyish rebellion towards my Dad's 'Do as I say, not as I do' attitude. He was very against illegal drugs, though he did enjoy a good drink. It was at this time of my life, at thirteen, that I tried my first cannabis joint. The area, though quite remote, had a reputation for drugs and one or two of my friends had been experimenting from the ages of eleven and twelve. I had always been told along the lines of:

"Don't do drugs, because they are very dangerous and can kill you", from my parents and I feared what my Dad would do if he caught me.

Still, I tried it anyway. In a rebellious moment, after a year or two of saying no, I decided what the hell. This was the turning point for me, where it all started; and I believe that had my Dad trusted me and not gone on at me so much, accusing me of taking drugs, etc, then I may not have rebelled and tried it.

However I don't blame him, for as an adult I am aware of how easy it is to get into and it could easily have happened anyway. It may have delayed me trying it, although what good this may have done is unknown. What happened, happened.

At one time during my teens, the area I lived had one of the worst reputations for drug use in Scotland. For the young there was little to do and it was easy to obtain hash, speed and LSD. Occasionally some grass would come over, but usually soap bar hash was the smoke, as it was called then.

Ecstasy was available towards my later teens but I never tried that until I was at college. I never did see it on the street as a teenager, but I heard of some using it at local raves, I think it was quite rare in those days and only the people close to the dealers would get any, or those that went to illegal raves.

Similarly was the case with cocaine and heroin. In those days we feared all hard class A drugs anyway.

Being only kids, most of us that dabbled, only tried hash and some of us tried the class A drug speed, or amphetamine sulphate, the dieting drug.

For it was so long ago that I tried my first joint, I have problems in remembering the feeling or effects. However it was the start of a long, long use of the drug cannabis, in it's varying forms.

It was not until the age of fourteen that I began regular use of Cannabis. We would roll up joints in the morning, on the back of the school bus and arrive at school mashed. Registration would be the worst, sitting there with red caned eyes and trying to look normal. My next door neighbour and one of my best friends, was in the year above me and we would sometimes have a joint on the beach, before the bus arrived.

My other best friend who lived a couple of villages away, was also a keen herbalist, we would smoke a joint out of my bedroom window sometimes. As my room was in the roof, the window would open upwards and out onto a slanted roof so the smoke would easily rise out into the fresh air without coming back in.

There was a beautiful view of the lochside out of this front window and many a night after school was spent smoking there, whilst I was meant to be doing homework, of course.

When we couldn't get any dope a cigarette would have to do and as Dad always left his tobacco in the same place in the kitchen it was easy enough to get my hands on. Soon enough I was addicted to the damn things and would be for a long time to come.

At fourteen I got a job delivering newspapers, and I used to deliver to approximately 170 houses over 2 miles. Some of the houses were on really steep drives and a long hike. It was a pain in the arse! But, it got me out of the house, as Dad was really strict about how late I could be out.

The delivery was only once a week, every Thursday, but it earned me £8 - £10 depending on how many additional leaflets there were.

Then there was my monthly living allowance from my Mum and Dad of £40, actually from Child Support Benefit. Mum and I agreed that I would buy all my own clothes and toiletries and stuff if I could have the money. This suited Mum as I have always had expensive tastes when it comes to clothes and trainers. So, there was £40/month plus £32 to £38/month from the paper round. That made me £72 to £78/month, which wasn't bad then for a teenager.

However, when the clothes were bought, I would save my money for booze, bought at lunchtime in town and sneaked back home in my school bag. My Dad's drinking habits influenced me greatly in these years and I grew up thinking that life was all about working hard, playing hard. His fast drinking I copied and his ability to hold so much alcohol was present also with my biological make up.

Looking back at life I believe these influential teenage years were vitally important for what was to follow. There is a saying that cannabis leads on to harder drugs and this I tend to agree with now. Alcohol played a large part in drug taking personally, as a lot of the times I tried something new, I was drunk. Remembering now that alcohol IS a drug itself.

Anything that intoxicates the mind and body is dangerous if not controlled and alcohol has the effect of loosening our self-control. It inhibits sexual desires, it prevents us from looking at potentially dangerous situations rationally and it induces high levels of energy, of which can be used negatively.

There were weekends in my rebellious years of fourteen and fifteen that we went camping up the woods at the back of the house, and sneaked booze out with us and cannabis and speed sometimes. I remember one era of my teens, probably at fifteen, when my friends and I stayed in our caravan outside the house some weekends, with a mini strobe light and radio one essential mix rave music blaring. I remember one night very clearly because we witnessed a serious car crash.

There were about four of us and we had all taken a wrap of speed, about a gram each, wrapped up in a cigarette paper and swallowed.

We had three or four girls with us but I don't think they were on speed, maybe drinking. We had decided to walk them back to where they were staying as they had missed the last bus, this was a journey of about two and a half miles.

As speed increases your energy we were happy to walk back too. However, when we returned we were walking down the main road, all of us feeling high, when a car raced past us, hit the wall on the opposite side of the road and veered into a tree. It exploded on impact and set the tree on fire. We were all shitting ourselves as we thought the driver had swerved to miss us.

Miraculously the driver got out alive, although with a broken arm, and ran off as he was drunk. The noise woke my Mum as this happened near the house, she ran out to find none of us in the caravan and thought we'd been involved in the crash. She was totally petrified. The police and fire brigade turned up and we had to answer their questions. The whole episode had made us paranoid, especially as we had taken drugs. Fortunately, neither Mum nor the police suspected that any of us were high, we were lucky, and the guy driving was even luckier. He had been going like a bat out of hell.

3 IN TRAINING

When I was on my weekly paper-round one evening I saw an advert on the front page of the local paper I was delivering. I couldn't miss it. Eighty places available in the Construction Industry Training Board.

I called the next day, applied for an application form and before I knew it obtained an interview down in Norfolk, all expenses paid.

Commencing in January 1996 after a sober Christmas, as Dad was off the booze, and a drunken New Years party at my best mate's house, college began. This was me leaving home. At the age of sixteen and a half it was a big move, although we would have accommodation at college. We were based there for six months before going to work on site with our sponsoring companies.

The college housed many practical training courses and was like a real building site with cement mixers, plant machinery for excavating, bulldozing, craning and piling.

You could learn scaffolding, bricklaying, plant mechanic and plant operating courses, and everything you can think of in construction. Part of our course included practical training where we had to carry out many construction techniques and practises including safety training and fire fighting.

As Norfolk was the opposite end of the country to my home I rarely came back. The train fare was about £80 return and we only got £50 per week that was spent on drink and hash mainly. There was a dealer in the local town whom the boys in college visited weekly and then dealt to us. In my second year, after my six-month work placement in London I got the contact and began dealing to my friends, but only friends, or people I could trust who would not grass me up if they got caught.

It paid for my hash intake which increased, as it was free. I was smoking about a quarter of an ounce a week and dealing about an ounce.

The dealer was a British bulldog type guy, heavy set, skin head; his front door was made out of steel and he lived in the top flat of a really dodgy area. Going to his house was a frightening experience at first, he was totally business and you could tell that he never smoked the stuff, just made money out of ripping off students like myself, as although I could make a free smoke, it was top dollar prices and we had nowhere else to go.

One night in my first year my friend Haggis from north Scotland scored a sheet of acid trips. About ten of us dropped one and were tripping our tits off all night. It was my second trip as I had tried half a tab in Scotland once.

That was the time a monkey came to life in a picture and talked to me! The poster had a picture of a monkey sat on the toilet, with the caption:

"It's Monday, what the fuck happened to the weekend?"

Only when I looked at the picture at my mate's house the monkey actually spoke the words to me. It was very strange.

The trip in college was a little different.

We were running through bramble bushes at one stage, and then when walking back to our accommodation block, the road turned into a river due to the amount of rain that was falling. Whilst walking down the street through the water it felt like I was going to sink down though the road as it resembled a river so much. Then we had to walk past a security guard who was exiting the block we were about to enter.

Our eyes wild, pupils big and black as night, with little or no colour in them. I remember looking in the mirror and imagining that I could see into my head through my eyes, it was scary stuff. We didn't have a bad trip but I believe the line between a good one and a bad one is very fine.

You could easily get paranoid or scared from the distorted reality you witness. It is best left alone as just one trip can send you insane. The insanity may not happen immediately after taking the drug, it may be years later. I've heard that more than seven in a lifetime can class you as clinically insane! ... I think for that reason I stopped at six, but finally went insane anyway.

On Thursday nights the local club held a girl's night where they got in free. We used to go there a lot, normally in big numbers as the locals hated the college boys as we used to get off with their women. Many a fight was had and I still to this day have war scars including a scarred lip and a broken nose from two different occasions. One night a local boxer smacked me whilst I was on the way out and bust my lip open, probably because I was chatting to his bird, it took twelve stitches to fix it up.

This was when my drinking began getting out of control. I would get so drunk that I didn't know what was going on. I began to realise that I was capable of aggressive acts of violence if in the company of others who were similarly drunk and of an aggressive nature. Realising that it was more the alcohol intoxication than the influence of others, my mood could rise and fall, depending on the vibe of the crowd I was with.

When sober I am not of a violent nature at all, but when drunk beyond control I can be a time bomb waiting to go off, if in the wrong company. Sometimes starting fights by saying the wrong things to people or acting like some kind of degenerate. Strange how alcohol degrades your personality, for some it is not so intense, but many can relate to similar less extreme experiences. Such as a loosening of the tongue, so to speak, swearing more and possibly adding a little tone to their dialect.

There were times when my mouth could have got my friends and I shot, had the people on the receiving end been armed. On a typical Thursday night ten pints or so were about average for me to down, sometimes with shots on the side. By the end of the night I could hardly walk never mind fight, yet we still got into them. It is of no wonder that I ended up battle scarred.

Growing up like this meant that I was going to learn the hard way, why could I not just do things in moderation and not get completely wrecked? Even then people advised you not to drink if in the wrong head space, but my head back then was always out of balance, I had no chance.

One week Haggis had been to London to see his brother the weekend before. He had come back with a single pill that he'd saved from his mental weekend of partying. This was my 1st attempt at taking ecstasy. We took half each and just watched the TV.

Not much happened except that the colours became deeper and more penetrative and I didn't really know what the programme was about. The next time I tried ecstasy was at the local club. Haggis was dealing the hash at college at this stage, and he saw someone from the dealer's house in the club.

He enquired about pills and scored. We took one each, came up quick which was fortunate as the club was nearly closing and we danced our tits off for the final hour.

Much later in life after becoming diagnosed as having mania I learnt what led me to become a cocaine abuser. The main cause was that I had been self-medicating with coke to try and stay sober. How ironic right?

Not knowing my life story the doctors could only advise and medicate the problem in hand, mania. So this book I hope will prevent some alcoholics from progressing their disease to drugs and to seek help early. Cocaine and cannabis abuse nearly killed me physically and brought on a psychosis that damaged me mentally and nearly brought me to suicide and accidental death, due to disorientation and a feather light grasp of reality.

Drugs, like alcohol are progressive, in the sense that once you have taken the first one or tried a drug a few times, your mind begins to change in relation to how dangerous it perceives the taking of drugs. You begin to think that 'Hey this ain't too bad, what was all the fuss about?' and 'I haven't become ill, I'm not dead, so why not do it again?' Your mind and body also become used to it, so that you need to take more to get the same hit.

Having been so lucky to be given another chance, I have told my story, to educate the addicted alcoholics, the addicted drug users, and their families about what can, and most likely will, happen if continued use goes on.

Until we get to that stage of my life, where reality changed and demons became 'real' we will continue to look into my progression of alcoholism and drug use until the demon drink became the demon coke and then visions and voices took over. The mind is a very clever thing and mind tricks can cause us to believe that these voices and visions are real, even making them so real that they become a part of your reality.

I think that if I were to slip back into a psychosis now, be it drug induced or of its own accord, I would be more sceptical of the origins of the voices and strange phenomena, and seek help from a psychiatric hospital. Whereas before, I believed that I was becoming telepathic and ran off from hospital twice, once before being sectioned under the mental health act and another time escaping from a secure ward in Basingstoke, during a section. Both times endangering others and myself, as I shall explain when we arrive at that episode of my journey.

On my return to college after the first year site placement in London, the money was better from the first year and every weekend was a complete bender. With more money to burn and burn it we did, you could imagine how we were gradually abusing our bodies more and more.

One weekend I went back to my mate's house in Wales. We smoked hash all the way there, went out drinking in his hometown that night, smoked some more when we got home and the next day got up and went to the pub for opening time at 9am and drank with his Dad. I remember it well, we won £150 on the gambling machine. Later that day we got the train to Liverpool, met up with our mate from Runcorn and another guy, who was scoring ecstasy pills and speed for us.

We were going to Creme in Liverpool, a famous house club with well known DJs. Paul Oakenfold, my hero at the time, was playing the 4am set. Like an idiot I got two pills and a gram of speed. One drug or the other would have been enough, I don't know why I got so much, greed I guess and lack of faith in the ecstasy, as at that stage I was a speed freak.

Looking back now we were so lucky not to overdose as I had only taken that one half ecstasy pill before in front of the TV with Haggis and then a whole one in the local nightclub but was pretty drunk then and it dulled the experience somewhat. I didn't realise then that the high depended on the environment.

Dancing brings you up and the high of going to Creme made the experience so intense, I vaguely remember being completely off my face and struggling to dance and walk properly, sweating intensely and creeping into paranoia from the strange looks from other clubbers. After the peak eased I relaxed and danced to Paul Oakenfold, unaware of where my mates were, probably still staring into space, dancing in another room.

You can very easily lose two to four hours when on ecstasy and have been dancing hard none stop without any water. This is how people get ill, even from clean, pure MDMA, the drug in ecstasy.

Drinking water is vital to survival. However remembering to drink is the problem. It's easy to forget when you last had a drink of water and some die from hydrating too much, again it's a fine line. The answer is, trust me, drugs are dangerous, if you're reading this thinking 'this guy sounds alright, he can't have experienced anything that bad, if he can tell this story'.... Think again.

If you are thinking of experimenting, bear in mind it only takes one bad trip or half a dodgy 'E' and you have brain damage, or un-repairable insanity where you know you are crazy but you can't snap out of it as you have lost control of your mind.

Or worse the birthday treat you give your friend ends in their falling to the dance floor in a coma, or dead, because of you.

How'd you live with that?

How do you tell their family?

I must stress that although the stories in this book may appear cool or inviting, they are not told to boast of a good time, they are told to enlighten you to the truth of what happens in life when you live it to the polar extremes… what goes up, must come down.

To understand the low, I think you need to understand the high. If you are already taking recreational drugs you will know that a comedown exceeds a hangover, so much so that I would get drunk all day following a night on drugs and let the hangover get me back to normal.

It was in this second year at college, when I was seventeen, that I got to know Stu. Check that, I wasn't even eighteen and I was drinking like a fish and abusing my body with other drugs. What a waste of life!

Some students in the first year opted for building studies and were in a different group than the civil students. Haggis chose building and although he was my best buddy in first year we lost touch as his building course finished a day or two after we started our second year.

Stu lived in London and he, Mick and I would get a lift back at weekends with our other mate Danny. Once in London I could catch a train to Swindon where my girlfriend from College lived. It was coincidental that Stu and I would become such good friends, in the first year I would get the train to London, then to Swindon and my work experience placement was just down the road, about two miles from Stu's house in west London.

4 THE OLD SMOKE

After my second year work placement in London, after completing college and passing my ONC, I was offered full time employment at the Precast Facility at Taylor Woodrow's headquarters, London, where I had spent all my work experience. I had chosen London because it was a base. If I had opted to go on various sites then I would have had to move all around the country. This would maybe have benefited me in terms of general construction experience, but I think I did just as well specialising in reinforced pre-cast concrete, and gained promotion quickly.

The usual way it works in construction, for people working away from home, is to arrive on site, check in with the Site Manager and then hunt out a B&B or ask around site for who knows of a house share wanted.

This was quite a daunting experience, not knowing where or who you are staying with, until the last minute. Although living in about five or six different suburbs of London and about seven different moves over five years due to the regular returns to college in Norfolk, I was very fortunate to find moderate lodgings and sound people. One of the houses I shared was with two guys from Sunderland, factory workers whom I knew and a Londoner, Big Joe, who owned the house.

He used to work in the factories before I started, but now he worked for the brewery as a long hauler. He would get kegs from his work that he kept in the back garden, he liked a smoke occasionally and because of this he was fine with me smoking in my room and occasionally in the living room, if he fancied a smoke too. His house was across the road from the works. Outside the works was a pub called The Civil Engineer, and we would go across to it often.

The first time I took cocaine was in The Civil Engineer with a friend of Joe's, on a night out. I had heard of this guy before as he used to work at the yard before I started, but was sacked due to being late and off sick a lot. Everyone knew he was a junkie. I asked him if he had any gear, meaning weed, as I had not had any for a while. He said no, but that he wanted some too, and that if we went halves he'd go get it. Excitedly I agreed, asked him how much he wanted: twenty five bucks. I had to borrow off Big Joe.

I never realised until he came back that down here gear meant coke, not hash, or maybe both, but it was cocaine he returned with. I thought I was getting a quarter hash for £25. A half ounce was £50 then, unless you dealt and it was cheaper.

Oh man I was pissed and although I had taken speed, acid and ecstasy before; this was a big step, and I knew it. I was worried and I spoke to Joe. He was a lot older than me, a big, tall fella. He kept his house clean and I respected him. He said he used to do cocaine sometimes. He was pissed too and said I'd be fine. He had one line that night and his pal and I snorted the rest of it in the toilets.

The Civil Engineer was also the place a short time later where I managed to meet someone to find a hash dealer after a couple of months of having no source. After playing hockey at the works sports centre I would have a few pints with the team then pop into the pub before crossing the road home. An Irish man asked me if I knew where to buy semtex in answer to my question on where to buy weed.

I cannot remember my answer exactly, but I think out of fear I made a comment about hearing stories of people in Glasgow where you could get it. Obviously, I had never heard anything of the sort. I think the man in the pub was just testing me, that I was not police. This era was the end of the IRA bombing campaign. The Omagh bombing was around this time and one of the last that I remember. During my school days in Scotland I remember at least once we had a bomb scare and had to evacuate the school. London was always on the news for tube strikes and I remember passing through London during one of these strikes when travelling from college to my parents, who now lived down south.

The night after meeting the Irish man, I was to meet another guy outside the pub, I turned up on time and after about fifteen minutes with no show, I was about to leave, when a man approaches me and asks if I want to buy any gear. He denied knowing the Irish man and said it was just a coincidence that he met me. Before he introduced me to the dealer he took me to his Mum's house where he lived, a block of flats at the back of the site I worked on and not far from the Civil Engineer pub. He had no cannabis in his house, but explained that he dealt in heroin and was waiting for someone to come and pick up a deal.

Looking back I now realise how dangerous this night was, how close I came to being a heroin addict. At the time I just thought I was being tested again, so to prove I wasn't police I accepted his offer to smoke some of the black liquid he was forming by burning the underside of a folded bit of tinfoil, with the brown speckled powder in it. He had a straw, or some paper rolled up like a straw, and was chasing the smoke as he gently tipped the foil from one side to another and let all the powder turn to liquid and be inhaled.

I think if it had been a needle I would have had to decline, but with not hearing of chasing the dragon before and seeing the powder, like cocaine but speckled brown, I thought a little try would not harm me. I spent a good couple of hours just sitting there watching the TV. It was so long ago I cannot recall anything in particular except I remember that the high was very subtle, unless I never took enough in. I remember the buyer coming to pick up his deal, it had been what we had been smoking.

Eventually we left his house and walked a ten to fifteen minute distance to the dealer's house, my source for the next few years in London. She was an old skinny looking woman with a big family. The house was always buzzing with her young sons in their late teens and early twenties. Their girlfriends, plus people waiting for their smoke, like me, would be there too.

Sometimes I'd wait sitting on their couch a while, saying nothing and watching the soap opera unfold. The family were obviously used to a full house, they would just act as if you weren't there. In fact no one spoke to you, so it was like you weren't there, and more like a fly on the wall. Usually they'd be drinking and smoking soap bar hash. It was always the same, as was their hash.

Dealers of this kind would buy what you call a nine bar (nine ounces) for maybe the price of six, I can't remember exactly. She would sell eighths, quarters and half ounces usually. On this first night my contact paid, I did not see the transaction and although I wanted a quarter I got an eighth with no change!

The morning after trying the heroin I felt sick as a dog and then I understood the danger. I realised that the only thing that would take away the pain was a short distance away, the guy was probably expecting me. Plus, he owed me £15 which was a lot of money to me at that time. After handing over £30 for a quarter, top prices, but I was too afraid to haggle with these people. The old lady dealer was probably not all that old but her face was wrinkled and she looked so frail, from years of abusing her body with alcohol, weed and heroin.

They were pleasant enough people really, only one of the younger sons seemed a bit wired, every time I was there, which became a weekly event. I waited a couple of days, it was the weekend and I had not had a smoke for ages,

I just stayed in watching TV, eating lots of munchies (chocolate, crisps and fizzy juice), probably had a few beers too but not as much as most weekends. The weed was my way of controlling my drink intake.

I was always on one or the other or both. I think it was the Monday that I knocked on the skag head's door. He wouldn't come to the door, probably had a spy hole; I went round all week. One night his Mum shouted that he was not there, but she didn't open either. This guy obviously ripped people off a lot and they were used to it.

The last time that I visited I had a bit of a shouting match and someone from the next door flat opened a window above me to see what was going on. It was the Head Quantity Surveyor from work, a senior man of high stature.

Shit, what was I to say? It was 10pm at least, maybe later, this guy worked away from home too and was probably going to bed or worse I had woken him up.

He shared digs with another manager. I apologised for the noise, said the guy owed me money from the pub. He seemed okay with that answer and I left, never to return. My £15 was smoked, never to appear again but at least I had made contact with the old lady for my weekly hash purchase. Eventually I figured it was well worth losing the fifteen quid, I had paid for the privilege of getting weed any night of the week, ten minutes from my digs.

This was an important, influential time of my life and although I never took cocaine again for another couple of years, it was the defining turning point in terms of whether I would. Had I not got myself into that situation with Big Joe and his pal, I may never have tried it, but now that I had I would not think it so dangerous in the future. Fortunately, I never came into contact with heroin again but I learnt how easily people can get hooked on that too.

There were many silly, drunken and drug infused nights to follow. Having gone back to college for three months then back to work for another nine months, I returned to college for the final visit in 1999.

During the first two weeks back, on a Monday night at the Chicago bar and nightclub where pints were just £1; I found myself dancing quite suggestively with two girls. I ask if they like my friend, who is at the bar, and would they like to come home with us. They agreed and so we left. Now this book isn't that kind of book, but you can guess what happened next, when I tell you my friend fell asleep after having not been used to smoking weed.

I met one of the girls a week or two later one night alone by chance, on the way home, and went back to her house. In the morning whilst letting myself out I found a bottle of methadone, prescribed no doubt for heroin. It dawned on me right there, that the first time we met I had not taken precaution in my eagerness to perform a long hoped for fantasy. The second thought was needles, the third HIV/AIDS.

It requires approximately one month, so I was told, for the disease to become apparent in the blood. I put off the thought of going for a test and eventually, some months later, when I started up with a new girlfriend I went for a test. On awaiting the results of the test, I experienced the longest week of my life.

Thankfully, I was in the clear and my lesson was learnt. Why did I have to push life to the extreme? Why not just take heed of what I read and heard in the news?

The following weekend I got very drunk having smoked far too much all day. Every day was the same. In fact, I don't know how I passed my course. In the meat market nightclub Manhattens with a lot less friends to back up any trouble than in the earlier years, I looked at the wrong girl again.

Unbeknown to me I was getting interest from her to make her ex jealous, who happened to be an ex-bouncer of the club. Two of his bouncer mates soon have my arms behind my back and allow him to come straight at me with a head butt to make a Glaswegian proud. My nose breaks, blood down my shirt again. 'Fuck, I hate this club', but karma is in play and I probably deserve it and before I know it I am being kicked down the metalwork fire exit stairs by the two big bouncers. Party's over.

When I get back to the Bed and Breakfast, disorientated and messed up I realise I gave my coat to a friend and in my coat pocket was the house key. With no money and having just staggered for over an hour from town I'm now on the edge of a bad housing estate with no shops or anything. It's approximately 4am on a very cold and frosty morning and I can't get in. I bang the door but no one comes. I try lying down on the frosty path but without a coat I am shivering like crazy. Will I die, I think, or just awake cold as hell?

Luckily the cold was too bitter for me to fall asleep and a plan came to mind. My friend Carl was staying in another house, renting a room from an old lady in the next estate. Carl had pulled a girl that night and hadn't come home. His landlady was still half awake expecting his return and heard me knocking on her front door. She kindly let me sleep in Carl's bed. Life saver!

That was our leaving party to celebrate the end of college. I went back to work with a messed up nose and two black eyes. Little was said. The guys at work knew by now that I was a head-case on the beer. A nice guy in the day, a raving drunk at every opportunity, full of fire and regret. There were emotional issues occasionally coming to the surface in some drunken chats, but as I didn't know how to deal with them; I continued losing myself and repeating destructive cycles.

I had moved back in to a flat I had stayed at before in London that was owned by a guy who operated one of the cranes on site. I was sharing a room with what I would call back then a *proper* alcoholic. This guy was a two number big three litre bottle of cider a night guy. That's nearly twelve pints every night.

Quickly my weight ballooned and I became a wreck. Now nineteen years old I've just become properly dependant on alcohol. Drinking every day and hitting it harder at the weekends, if you can believe that possible?

Addiction ruled my life, from drink, smoke, cannabis, to sex. I had a thirty year-old girlfriend in London who had a little boy. I would come back from a weekend seeing my long term girlfriend in the West Country and stop in to see my girl in London. Well she wasn't quite my girl, she knew about my girlfriend. She had a crazy ex-husband in the army who was the father of the wee man.

This girl in London was really hot and big into her smoke. I remember hearing about Princess Diana's death one early morning when it happened, I was still sitting up finishing my joint and watching telly. The girl in London soon got fed up with my other life and the fact I was letting myself go. My long term girl let herself go at the same time, and was getting fatter by the week. We would sit around drinking vodka and orange from around 11am, then smoke weed, then have sex, then do it all over again all weekend, with lots of munchies and films in between.

What a waste of life. Maybe, looking back, we were just depressed with how our lives had turned out. We both had serious issues and regrets from our youth too. Our parents were messed up and now we were going the same way.

Fortunately for me my flat mate left the company and got a job back in his hometown far away. I started going to the gym and then I decided to change the squalor I lived in and found a room share in a semi-detached house in a nicer area. I moved in to a single room with two single Irish girls and a guy from Stoke on Trent. The girls had been in London a few years like me. One did her diploma in nursing in west London and worked in a local hospital, the other worked for a marketing company, I think, and the guy worked for an airliner. It was a positive change.

I was cycling three miles to work, going to the gym at lunch time and cycling home. I finally got a semi-grip, curbed my addictions to a semi-controlled status and attracted the attention of the ladies. I fancied the nurse the most and we finally got together one night following a doctor's party. By the way, doctors and nurses are the worst for drug and alcohol abuse.

We pilled it up on several occasions at their parties. Ecstasy was dropped into your glass, you saw it and went, 'fuck it', dropping the whole pill in one. Usually I would take half first and give it a chance, always in fear it may be a bad one, like the ones you heard about, killing people in clubs. You always hoped that by taking only half you may have a chance of getting better should you take a funny turn. Probably not a good philosophy. I've had some of my maddest experiences from just halves; it's just as toxic, believe me. You are either up or down. It's like alcohol, the first pint is the best, the rest is a catch up to try and put you back on the level you were enjoying so much.

Between the crazy nights out, I worked hard, I took a second job in a pub along the road and I did my driving test. Although on my first driving lesson I was on a come down from ecstasy. I lived life on a knife edge and I knew it. I wasn't for calming down though, life was intense and so many around me did the same, if not to the full extent as I did. I was excessive and renowned for it.

Out of all my friends if anyone was going to bend the brain and nervous system to as far as it could yield it was going to be me, I knew this too, but you just don't think it's going to happen to you. Also, you have no fear because you think that if it does happen you won't know much about it. Wrong on both accounts.

The pub work, as you can imagine was probably not the best move for a young alcoholic. I rattled every drink bought for me after each shift and then bought a couple more and cycled home. Home at 1am, then cycle to work at 6am for a 7am start, work twelve hours to 7pm and cycle back home. Fortunately, shifts were staggered with one at the weekend.

My first shift was a Sunday afternoon and I nearly never went back following a massive punch up in the main bar. I heard the landlady screaming as I was serving in the lounge bar, I ran through into the main bar and chaos was a mild word for what I saw before me. I've seen enough bar brawls when drunk and been part of a couple too, but it's a different story when you're stone-cold sober.

Two men throwing their arms around trying to grapple and punch each other, with the landlady like cheese in a sandwich between them. All around were other men, shouting and trying to break it up. I ran around the bar and dived into the crowd, pushing my way into the thick of it, grabbed the nearest guy and dragged him out into the street.

He was so stunned he didn't try and fight back, but as I turned to go back in, an older man, his father I believe, came at me aggressively. I ran back around behind the bar and the landlady ran upstairs to call her husband who was eating his Sunday lunch.

The father then chased me behind the bar and kept coming, following me through into the lounge bar. We ran out towards where the older punters were sitting around tables quietly enjoying their drinks. The father threw a punch at me, I ducked then pushed him back, he stumbled and before he recovered I tried explaining that I work here. He wasn't having any of it, his eyes were glazed in drunken hatred and he looked like he wanted to kill me.

I turned, not wanting to get into a full blown fight, and as I tried to get away he grabbed my shirt. It was a tight, short sleeve shirt that was actually my Dad's when he was a similar age. It tore straight off my back as I turned quickly to face him half naked, and hold my ground. I just stared at the maniac waiting for his next move. No one from the pub intervened.

Just at the moment I faced the guy ready to go into full blown attack as my last defence, as he stood with the exit behind him; the landlord came from nowhere and jumped in between us. He was a big, hard man from Scotland and was used to trouble. The crazy father tried to protest and the landlord backed me up and made him believe that I had just started work that day, and that he wouldn't stand for fighting in his pub.

Needless to say, the guy was barred. However, he didn't go quietly, swearing to get me when I finished work. It was a long afternoon and evening, but fortunately despite my worry that a crowd would be waiting for me, I saw no one as I shot out of the back door on my bike, riding as fast as possible.

I did go back three days later for my next shift and there was no trouble after that. In fact, I feared some of the lounge characters rather than the lager louts next door, after learning that many were old gangsters. Some of them were real characters, lifeless eyes and hard as nails.

Crime was and is everywhere and these people have been in it a lifetime. They can have you in a body bag in the blink of an eye, and as I have always been quite street-wise and aware of my surroundings I missed little.

You learnt to ask no questions, offer no friendly chat unless you were spoken to and just be quick and polite about your business, serving pints and clearing tables. My manners and privacy earned me a good many drinks. These guys weren't tight with their money and they liked to flash the cash between themselves, like Gorillas banging their chests; mine is bigger than yours kind of thing; I'm the hardest animal in the jungle today.

The saying 'ignorance is bliss' is so true. Although awareness might just stop you putting your big foot into affairs and keep you out of trouble. There was a South African barman serving the main bar sometimes. He was blissfully ignorant and his ego was only untouched because of it. He had no fear, for a posh university student.

He was doing a Masters in Construction Management, a very far away goal for me at that time, I barely had the intellect and short term memory to complete college. In fact at that time I had no desire to learn or progress, just get high. I wasted a good part of ten years with that narrow minded philosophy.

Maybe it was partly an age thing. I always thought I looked older and acted more mature than I was, but over the years I've noticed people at similar ages to me back then progressing in their careers much faster than I ever did. It is evident that drug and alcohol abuse slows down development, especially as our minds are still developing into our early twenties.

Would it have made any difference to my life back then had I realised this?

No, probably not. Maybe you will be different, or be able to get through to your son, brother, sister or friends who are abusing themselves and creating a complicated web of deceit that is founded on their lies to themselves, so deep and denied that they don't believe that there is a problem.

Each individual is different and so I can't advise how you awaken someone, but I have found that subtle hints help better than plain statements. It's a case of un-clearing the path for them and letting them walk along it themselves. You cannot push somebody down a path unwillingly, they need to want to go, or they don't. If you force someone through threat or otherwise, expect an equal or greater resistance with a final outcome worse than the position you currently find yourself in as a bystander.

Sometimes the only way is to not care and let the person find their own way, it must be the hardest thing to do when all you can do is hope or pray that they won't come to serious harm before realising that they need help. I was never really on this side for long, I have tried to help people so I know a little of how this feels, but from the way I fought my loved ones who tried to help me, I can see now what it must have been like for them.

With me on a path to self destruction, another aid came on the wind of change. The pre-cast concrete facility that I worked in was to close, and all employees were to be made redundant, including myself, despite being sponsored for the last four years through college.

We all undertook redundancy training and looked for new jobs. It was the dawn of the millennium, we were not in a full blown recession but new jobs were not abundant.

The main advice was to be completely flexible in terms of location. If you are prepared to travel you have a better chance of getting a new job, the freelance consultant preached. Gather all your contacts and grow your network. In the days of no social media this included your address book, email contacts and going to every supplier, client, previous employer, colleagues and students you had met.

Finally, after many enquiries, a small company in Chester showed an interest in me. Some things are just meant to happen and this was one of them.

5 CHESTER RACES

The most dangerous experience on ecstasy was when my best mate visited me in Chester when I first moved and we went to London for a weekend. We stayed with my girlfriend who still lived there whilst looking for a job near me. My girlfriend and her best friend from back home, who lived with her now, came with us for the start of the afternoon, but we soon left them looking around the tourist places and shops. My mate and I went on a pub crawl of London's old bars where we took a substantial amount of cocaine washed down with copious amounts of beer, and finally went to Camden, to the Camden Palace, a club in an old theatre that my college mate Stu had introduced me to with his buddies.

We took pill after pill. They were easy to get back then in the club. We had 4 each and we were still not coming up. The charlie had sobered us up, but we weren't high anymore. I figured the charlie may have been preventing the ecstasy to work, I hadn't mixed them before.

Almost considering going home then BANG, a quadruple drop hits us both like a freight train and then another bang, the night was over. We dropped another three pills each that night to keep the buzz going, seven in total; and at the end of the night we stood together under a little archway smoking fags and watching younger people than us, it seemed, dancing a new dance. Five or six am and a select few, cool-looking young ones, who hadn't completely fried their minds, and who's legs weren't jelly like ours, were dancing casually with a swaying of the hand in what appeared to be in unison, like they were all part of the same gang. Maybe they were, maybe they weren't. Reality was blurred. The come down had arrived in force. It was past time for getting home and we had a long way to go from Camden to outer west London.

We made it home completely withdrawn. Looking back now we weren't far away from the clutches of the blue blanket, the type that the police give you when you get brought into the psychiatric hospital from whatever nightmare you have been living.

The worst thing was we had heard of the pills we were taking, the first four that we thought were duds were white oval tablets speckled with brown spots. Rumour on the street was they were laced with heroin and they had been referenced to killing people on the news. The fact is ecstasy is always in the news for killing people, it's sometimes a bad batch but usually it is just the personal reaction to the MDMA drug and what it's cut with. It creates heat exhaustion and can cause heat stroke if takers do not hydrate and chill out regularly.

The following week we finished the rest of the charlie, out nearly every night in Chester. My mate pulled twice that week and he was having a good time. He crashed the Chester college fresher's week, managing to get us both into the union one night.

With me working away during the week days and my girlfriend on shift work at the local hospital, working weekends, it wasn't long after she moved in with me that we drifted apart, living separate lives. I became depressed unless I was out drinking and I think half the time I went out I was just lonely and bored. I started drink driving.

It crept up on me after living with my Granddad for a couple of months before I found somewhere to live, as he had drunk drove all his life from when it was not illegal. He had lost his license one New Year's eve a few years prior, but that still had not deterred him from having two or three cars and still driving under a ban. And still driving under the influence, during and after the ban was lifted.

My job required me occasionally to drive to Scotland at the start of the week. If my girlfriend was working at the weekend then I would sometimes go on Saturday and get a night out in Glasgow with my mates. On Tuesday or Wednesday I would head down to Hull, stay there for a night, where I partied like a student in a great bar next to a French hotel. A bottle of red with my meal, all on expenses, then off to the student bar and maybe a club afterwards with some group of random students.

The following week I would go to my projects down south, usually get Great Yarmouth out of the way first and then sometimes to London. I had about three to five projects going on at any one time and much of my working week was spent driving. On average I could bag some seven hundred miles per week.

I was really bad for smoking weed and driving too. I used to smoke joints like cigarettes back then. Somehow I managed not to fall asleep at the wheel, or get caught by the police. The projects in Scotland, Hull and Great Yarmouth were major power stations and not the places to be hung over or high on weed, as I often was during the day.

In terms of co-ordination it made me slow down and alertness wasn't really a problem. Not like being drunk at the wheel, where reaction times are slow compared to increased speeds from over confidence. Still it was a dangerous and irresponsible bad habit.

One weekend the drink driving really hit a new level. Upon leaving a club with a couple I didn't know, and another girl in the front seat, I took a roundabout too fast and smashed straight into a lamppost.

Either the girl or guy in the back seat was not wearing a seat belt. Anyway one of them broke their nose on the front head rest. They were both screaming and making a scene and threatening to call the police, so I made sure all of them were okay and then took off. As actually advised to do, by a lady who came out of her house and was trying to calm the girls down.

I don't remember how I got home. Luckily, I took a note of the street where I crashed and the following morning I called the roadside assistance company. A tow truck picked me up and took me to collect the car and take it to the garage. Fortunately, the car was still where I abandoned it; I was worried it was going to have been found already by the police. As the police did not get involved I filled out an insurance form at work, making up a story about a dog running in front of the car, causing me to swerve and hit a lamp post.

No one at work questioned the claim and all was well. Did I learn my lesson though? Course not. Some weeks later in a new car, I took off into central London after an evening on the beers in south London, with some guys from work. I had an ecstasy tablet in the car and the drink had given me a great idea to take a joyride into the city, find a club and neck the pill. I was on my own. I parked on the edge of Leicester square and went into a small club I had been into before. There was only about an hour and a half left, the bouncer said. "That'll do", I thought. I bought a bottle of beer, went to the toilet and took the whole pill.

The music was pretty tame, it was early mid week and the dance floor was quiet, but I came up and the place picked up, or at least in my head it did. All of a sudden everyone stopped dancing. I thought for a second there was a fight or someone had collapsed. No commotion though. Then I realised that people were staring upwards. There was at least one television in the corner of the ceiling, pretty strange for an underground nightclub. On the screen there was a boxing match going on or at least had been. One of the guys was holding his ear and blood was running down his face.

It was Evander Holyfield, and Tyson had just bitten a chunk out of his ear!

I straightened up after that. Not many danced afterwards either, so I made idle chat with a couple of girls, but I could hardly put three words together.

We left the club together and once I knew they were not old bill, I offered them a lift home. They took me up on the offer, which was odd when clearly I was off my head, but still, they probably were too. Anyway, having drove in the opposite direction to where I wanted to go, I dropped them somewhere north. They never offered me in, but for some reason they stole my wash bag, with designer aftershave in it, that had been sitting on the back seat.

I headed south, back through the city and just as about to take a left and cross the river, I get flashed by a speed camera. At the time I didn't think much of it. One night coming down from Scotland to Hull along the A1, I was flashed about four separate times, again half pissed, and no notice came in the post. So I probably hoped the camera was not loaded with film. No such luck, a speeding ticket arrives to my company address, taking me up to six penalty points on my license, three from this event and three from running a red light in Chester.

Now you can usually hold up to twelve penalty points before losing your license. However, I didn't realise that if you get six within the first six months of passing your test then you have to re-sit your test. My six months were not up were they, so I had to cycle to work and get the train or lifts to sites for a couple of months whilst I re-sat my test.

The company was like John Grisham's *The Firm,* corrupt as fuck, and the owner drove a Porsche at high speed everywhere he went and had a major drinking problem. So my little escapades were not queried, and deemed to be, just what they looked like on the surface, speeding fines, etc.

I would like to say that losing my license calmed me down a little, but in reality I don't think it did. The same pattern of experiences continued, including drunken excursions to Liverpool to drop E, after drinking in Chester. They were never planned events but spur of the moment decisions, after alcohol had corrupted my mind.

Some normality in life came from a good work-found friendship, a guy who lived on the Wirral between Chester and Liverpool. He was married and they had a lovely house and invited me over for dinner occasionally. We also went on couple's nights out when my girlfriend wasn't working. My new sane mate and I went fly fishing a few times, after I gave him one of my fly rods, some flies and tackle. His first trout on the fly was about three and a half pounds, it fought for ages and he was as happy as a pig in shit. We drank a couple of cans and smoked a spliff or two on the boat and it was good company.

That day he caught his fish he let me drive his Porsche. It was ten years old, an old style 911, not like the bosses bran new one. It was amazing though and I've wanted one just like it ever since. The fishing rods fitted in the bonnet and the engine roared in the rear as we shot along at nought to sixty in a matter of seconds. What a buzz.

After a year of quantity surveying, work dried up and there was only enough work for the Senior QS. Despite my nightly antics I always got to work on time and when I was there I worked hard. And so it paid off, for the boss didn't want to lose me. Instead, he thought that a spell in the accounts department would be good for me and they had a new accounts software that they needed someone with construction knowledge to assist with, coding up the ledgers to illustrate site spending, etc.

So I moved to the back of the office with the accounts girls where my new boss I think was into me. She kept asking me out for lunch and we had a couple of beers and chatted about nothing in particular. I felt like I could have made a move on her had I wanted to, but despite my occasional drunken straying when fed up in my relationship, or thinking my girlfriend was cheating on me, the usual me was not like that. Her husband sounded like a good guy too. I didn't know about karma then, but I did have some morals when sober.

The cash flow forecasting was interesting, but I wasn't happy in the role, mainly because the company really was like Grisham's The Firm. However, I did have fun looking into their accounts, where £200K value jobs had cost £1M plus and the bank debt always stayed at around £2million in the red, no matter what revenue was coming in.

From dire boredom, mainly from purchase-ledger entries and being stuck in one chair all week, I got in with some students in Chester and it was a bad move, they had drugs all the time and were out every night. Drink driving and taking drugs became my normality, previous episodes had evidently just been in training.

I had always wanted to work abroad and with lots of time to think in the office and not being happy in my new role, I searched for jobs on line. The first job I applied for abroad was in Barbados and within a day I was contacted by a youngish Scottish lady in London. She was leaving to get married and have children, it transpired, and she wasn't interested in obtaining lots of candidates. So she said she liked my CV, liked my attitude and thought I was the guy for the job and closed the advert! It all sounded too good to be true.

The company in Barbados liked my CV and experience too. They paid for her to fly out there. I posted her pictures and drawings of the jobs I was working on, for her to take with her. I think in truth the company liked me because I wasn't degree qualified and they could pay me less and it looked like I was capable.

I was flown out there myself for an interview, put up in a top class hotel and wined and dined for the long weekend. We visited some jobs on the Friday and went clubbing that night. On the Saturday I was taken out in the owner's luxury yacht, not the sail type but the speed boat type that you can fish off the back and drive from up top or inside. We caught Barracuda and King fish whilst drinking the local *Banks* beer from eight in the morning until midday, and then retired inside and drank *Mount Gay Barbados* rum.

On the way home the boss stopped into the *Boathouse* beach bar near the capital, Bridgetown and we drank some more rum and ogled the women, then he drove me home to my hotel. I had already purchased some local green on the beach of my hotel with some Rasta made bracelets for my sisters the previous evening. Obviously, the weed was not for them.

A joint or two later and I was out for the count. Sunday I caught a flight home via Miami. I took a taxi to South Beach from the airport, had a crap pint of Guinness in an Irish bar then checked the beach babes out and got another taxi back to the airport. I still had hours to pass whilst waiting for my night flight, so I drank vodka cocktails then finished the weekend off with a couple of quarter bottles of wine on the plane. It was a long way to go for a weekend but what an experience. I loved it, and I was bought, Barbados had me.

A month or so after my interview and it was Christmastime. My girlfriend and I went to Scotland for New Year, having planned to stay in a hotel in Glasgow with a best friend and his partner, but unfortunately he got an eye infection and was in hospital.

We went out in Helensburgh instead, where he lived, and another best friend was out with us. Having been a little frustrated and disappointed that my other best mate couldn't make it and was in hospital my mood wasn't quite in the zone it should have been.

I drank too much then accused my mate of trying it on with my girlfriend even though he was just dancing with her. I still had hang ups about my previous girlfriend's desires to sleep with him and me together and also, when we were at school, not all that long before, he went out with a girl I had fancied since first year. At this stage I wasn't consciously annoyed with him about it, but later self analysis of my feelings brought it to my attention.

I'll not imply that such self reflection of feelings is easy, nor deny that I only did it when at my lowest of lows, but I can confirm that by recognising the feeling for what it is, understanding it and forgiving the persons, the factors/situations and any other causes, including ones self pity and other self caused factors; is the best way to let go and free oneself of recurring associated negative feelings.

Following the self analysis of my feelings, I communicated my issues to my friend. This all occurred some years later, but I found that by recognising the negative feeling that had come out in different forms, but mainly anger, and then communicating this to him directly I was able to forgive, and ask forgiveness from him for my subsequent behaviour.

In doing so our friendship was rekindled from an honest platform, allowing clean air between us from then on. This philosophy has worked for me many times since, but sometimes one of the people involved fails to continue to uphold the chance to maintain a friendship of honesty and freedom of speech, and that causes new feelings of doubt and subsequent negativity.

If such a thing keeps recurring, then walk away, put some miles between you, whether geographic or just mentally, but guard yourself from feelings of negativity where possible, especially when it becomes apparent that showing your cards is just causing you to be taken for granted.

It's easier to say, 'oh so and so is worse than me', and to continue living a bad lifestyle. It happens a lot.

Thinking that you're superior, when in fact, you are in denial, prevents you from opening up to yourself in honesty to work through your problems.

Reaction, and unaware reaction in particular, is a major factor in maintaining self abusive behaviour. This is often followed by denial and further events can complicate and shroud the true cause of a problem, creating a web of deceit. This is very important to understand, as the reality of which is the main cause for the build up of chaos.

For anyone treading along on this path, a breakdown is inevitable.

So as the new years party nears it's end, I grab my car keys and head out of my mates flat. On route to Glasgow to see my cousins, who are still partying I'm sure, my mobile phone rings and just as I answer I see flashing lights ahead of me. Thinking it is the police I brake hard.

Unbeknown to me, due to obvious reasons for lack of awareness, the road is icy, it's four am, Hogmanay, Scottish New Years Eve, in fact News Years day morning now to be correct.

My friend who had called my phone to see if I'm okay had recalled afterwards, hearing an awfully loud smashing noise that went on for a couple of seconds, and then silence. I never did find the phone, maybe it flew out of a smashed window, but the car had flipped and rolled through two sign posts before landing back on its wheels and facing in the opposite direction on the embankment.

The roof was completely squashed in, except for the driver's seat, no air bags went off, the driver's door opened easily, and I just stepped out. The boot was jammed open, I reached in grabbed my trainers, changed my boots, left the crate of alco-pops someone had given me and made a run for it.

A guy tried to talk to me and I just kept running, although at first in the wrong direction. Upon realising this I turned around and ran past the scene.

Later I found out that the tow truck driver, from the flashing lights I'd seen he was rescuing another car that had skidded on the ice more than likely, was to testify that I had been drinking. There was also a taxi driver who witnessed the crash from the sliproad to a bridge just ahead, he had collected me and gave me a lift to Glasgow. He also was to testify.

When the taxi driver asked me where I had been, I made up a story about walking from a party in the last town in the direction I had just come from. When I arrived at my cousin's my chest was starting to hurt. It turned out I had bust a couple of ribs. I asked him to text my girlfriend to say I was okay and I grabbed a beer and took a line of coke, not from my cousin who abstained, but from an unnamed guy in the flat; and all was well again until the morning.

The next day I called the insurance and sorted a hire car. I drove to meet my girlfriend and her friend who was with us and gave them the car to drive home. I then stayed in Scotland, got a solicitor, went to the police with a made up story and got my belongings from my impounded car.

Some months later a notice came in the post for me to attend court for suspicion of being under the influence of drugs or alcohol. Although I needed to learn a proper lesson in life, luck would have it for me at that time that the taxi driver had failed to attend court.

I applied for another license, a copy, stating that mine had been lost. I did this because I fully expected a driving ban, and a paper copy licence was all I needed for a driving licence in Barbados. At the time, that was all I was concerned about.

All of this stress just made life more complicated and things became unmanageable. I finally gave up my job following a promise that my visa to Barbados would arrive any day, it didn't and after a month of fly fishing, drinking and smoking on the other days, and running out of money; my old boss asked me if I would consider returning on a temporary basis, weekly paid, to manage the construction of a roofing contract for a hospital in Birmingham.

I could just about travel it daily at one and a half hours each way, and stayed over some nights, all expenses paid. I got another company car and that was it for the next six months or so. Problem was I was too young and too addicted to illegal substances and alcohol to deal with the stress that the managing of this project caused me. I had managed projects for two weeks at the most on my own, in absence of Project Managers, but this particular job was one of two managed by one Project Manager.

He focussed on the larger job down the road and I was left to run with the other. At just under £1M it was complicated enough, a curved roof, with three levels in a semi-circle, the top and bottom curvature was made from welded, hipped Aluminium Seam joints.

A health and safety plan and safe method of works was in place when I arrived and the decking had just started. The main contractor was nervous because the Health and Safety Executive had issued a local work at height blitz for the region. In other words they had promised to visit all potentially high risk projects with regards to working at height, with the capacity to close the site down should it not be compliant with current legislation.

The client had us amending method statements by introducing further risk controls such as men attached to harnesses and inertia reels, that allow them to walk to unprotected edges and should they fall, they suspend from an automatic locking system on the reel that prevents further wire extending.

However, there was scaffold edge protection all around the perimeter of the roof and a safety net system underneath the work face areas. This control method was usually all that was required, as it was standard industry practice and recognised by the HSE.

Yet on one, not so fine day for me, the HSE did arrive and they raised the question no one was looking for. They enquired about the safety net system to an overhang on the inner circle of the roof. They wanted to know if we could prove by means of calculation that the nets could withhold the weight of a man should he fall, as the netting was fixed to secondary steel work at every other spacing. Usually, good practise is to fix the nets to stronger primary steel work throughout.

There was no way to prove it and so we received a prohibition notice, which meant all works stopped to that area of the roof, which really was fortunate because the whole site could have been shut down. Nevertheless, it was an embarrassment to the sub-contractor I worked for, and for me, as this was their first notice served. My defence was that the netting had been installed before I arrived. The other PM was fully aware of the set up but I didn't mention this as it was obvious.

Although I was backed up by management and known for being diligent in health and safety; dealing with the stress of the issue on top of the stress of man management, caused me my first breakdown.

It wasn't a breakdown per say, but I did admit I was an alcoholic and this occurred following a holiday with my girlfriend that was paid for by the steel scrap money I made on site. Another stress factor because the guys argued over the splitting up of the cash.

We were flying back from Tenerife, joints had been smoked at the poolside earlier that day, always better to drink then smoke, that way you usually whitey or go to bed, the other way you get more drunk; and I drank at the pool. I drank in the airport and I drank on the plane. I got so drunk that I spilt red wine on a passenger next to me and completely embarrassed my girlfriend. You might be wondering by now, how on earth is she still my girlfriend!

When we landed in Manchester, I blacked out, not fainting, which would have been much better, but more a kind of being possessed is the best way to describe it. I've seen it in others many times, eyes glaze over, face is determined, actions are erratic and anything can happen. Memory loss often ensues, which for the alcoholic is bad in the sense that they don't realise how bad their actions were, which means they are less likely to stop it re-occurring.

For some unknown reason, I started being cheeky to the armed police who were patrolling Manchester airport, as this was a time shortly after 9/11. The situation quickly worsens, with me getting violent and out of control and I am arrested in front of lots of witnesses.

The embarrassment I caused my, I'm sure you can believe it, now ex-girlfriend was unforgivable and hence, after a night in the cells beating myself up trying to kick the steel door down, I owned up to carrying serious personal issues, amongst which was alcoholism. That was the only condition I thought I knew how to start tackling and so I started going to Alcoholics Anonymous (AA).

The meetings were two or three days a week, or if you travelled you could attend one every day. But the first mistake I made was to insist I wasn't giving up cannabis and that I didn't have a problem with that because it wasn't addictive. Well obviously I was addicted, if there are no addictive properties in weed then at least anything that takes your mind to a place you deem happier, is deemed addictive.

So one or two meetings a week kept me off alcohol, for a while at least. It was difficult and I tried my best. In fact, I lasted a month or two. I can't remember how long exactly, but in the August of 2003, around the time of my twenty third birthday, I flew out alone to Barbados.

6 BARBADOS AND THE WEST INDIES

On my first arrival at the island, for my interview, I was surprised at how flat Barbados was and how many tin-roofed shacks there were, but I was pleasantly surprised with how green it looked. The rainy season had not long ended, it was around late November, early December, and although there is no seasonal climate as such on the equator, the drier months, with slightly longer days of maybe an extra hour, had arrived.

On my second arrival for the start of my three year work visa, it was mid to late August. The island's vegetation was not as I remembered it, it was browner and no deep greens, as before. Although this was just my impression from the airplane coming into land. In fact, around the island there would have been plenty of green, such as the large banana plant leaves.

I was lonely on arriving, the third world look to the place was a stark contrast to the old Cheshire stone-built houses and ancient city statues, cathedral and surrounding old roman stone wall; the kind of scenery I had been used to for the last two years.

Would my heart settle I wondered? Indeed it took some months, three that I remember. It wasn't the fact that I was on an island, although the more I got to know the island the more it felt like I was contained. It was the culture change that hit me the most. I suppose I fitted in quickly because I like outdoor living, the sea, and the beach. And the people there were very friendly and welcoming.

With the exception of the main towns, most of the population live in wooden shacks with tin roofs and generally have little income. Paid work is in short supply for such a great population, of around approximately 284,000 over approximately 166 square miles, though some 80,000 live around the capital Bridgeport, on the south-east coast.

Many of the young lads, and the odd lady I may tell you about later; make their living on the beaches. Some in fair legal trade, such as bead chains, bracelets and the like, or offering massages or jet-ski hire and other water sports. Many sell weed, charlie, crack and some will try to take you out and show you a good time; they expect a few drinks for the privilege. Some guys try their luck with the ladies, often the older ones, I think in a vain hope to marry, or at least to visit them on holiday back at the tourist's homes. Some are successful, more than I would have believed possible.

For the first weekend I was in the same hotel that I stayed in for my interview. This was in the South of the island, near St Lawrence Gap, where the biggest nightlife district can be found. On my first evening, after having something to eat, I bought a coffee and sat at the bar. It was pretty quiet for a Saturday night I thought. However, nightlife in Barbados doesn't start until around 12am, and although the hotel was within a busy nightlife district, it was surrounded by thick green canopies of trees and bushes. So many big green-leafed plants and trees and little frogs whistling, which sounded like crickets.

The first time I visited I didn't realise how close I was to the party zone, which was probably a good thing, or I may have missed my flight home!

An English girl of Indian descent comes to the bar to order drinks and starts a conversation with me. She is wondering why I am alone and drinking coffee, so I tell her my story and, probably feeling sorry for me being on my own, invites me to meet her friends, including another English girl and a local black guy with dreads.

The girls, who's names I now forget, were over on a hockey-playing holiday, from Staines, in England. They had met the Rasta looking guy on the beach, a regular beach bum who chatted them up. He was a sound guy though and a pretty trustworthy character for a beach bum, we got on well. It turned out they were heading out to the Gap for beers and asked if I wanted to go along.

So, I did, and it wasn't long before my abstinence from alcohol was broken. I had lasted maybe an hour in the bar before taking my first drink. So obviously that was it for me, if I couldn't last the first night there wasn't much chance.

That first evening Rudeboy Rasta supplied me with some cocaine. It was very strong and I took too much of it and can't remember much else about that first night. The second night I think I kissed the girl I had been talking to, at least I know I did the following night after that because we went for a drive. She told me she had never taken charlie and that she was a virgin. She wanted to change both of these things! I wasn't keen on being the one to give her coke, I knew how it worked, I told her as much and she respected me for it.

Now we could have changed the other thing whilst I was staying at the hotel, but they didn't let me in that night, because they knew I had checked out. It was Monday now. I had moved into a house on the west coast, in a place known as Sunsetcrest, Holetown, in the parish of St James.

It was too far to drive her back there, then drop her off at the hotel, go home and then go to my first day at work later that morning, so we tried it in the car, but it was too hot and didn't feel right, and so I drove her back to her hotel.

Most of my working week consisted of sitting in a cold, air conditioned office, looking out of the tinted windows, wishing I was on the beach! Luckily I couldn't see the beach as the office was inland. I got friendly with a real Rastafarian, who was a draughtsman at my work. We would take turns going to his, or mine, at lunchtime to have a Rasta Caribbean lunch, consisting of natural weed, usually of St Vincent origin and sometimes a bottle of strong stout each, such as Guinness or similar, six or nine percent proof.

I was keen on Guinness before I went to Barbados, it was my regular tipple in Cheshire, but I had never tasted Guinness Foreign Extra Stout. It is a Caribbean brew, originally brewed and shipped from Ireland, from 1801, for the Irish labourers working in the West Indies. It was g-o-r-g-e-o-u-s, my Rasta pal couldn't understand why I drank it so quickly, but then he wasn't an alcoholic.

To begin with at weekends I was hanging with my beach bum Rasta-like Rudeboy mate, who introduced me to big B, who was constantly in and out of jail for dealing drugs. I was aware of the danger and I knew I took a risk hanging out with these guys and also I knew I couldn't trust them, but I always try and take people on face value and give them a chance.

I had little to lose but my freedom and hanging out like that does actually help you adapt to your surroundings quickly; it only became a worry when I took too much coke and became anxious. That happened again, on my second weekend; at a club called Bakoo, in Holetown, not far from my house.

I let the guys stay over that night. My beach bum, rude boy mate, looked the Rasta part, with long black dreadlocks. Despite his grownup approach and wisdom-appearing nature, which may have come about from his experiences in New York, where he had actually brought back a gun from and talked of his time in a gang there. He was far from Rasta in reality, not that I yet knew true Rastafari, but in the short talks with my Rasta friend from work, I had glimpsed the deepness and honesty of their ways to know the difference.

As the persona of rudeboys is usually the image the holiday makers mistakenly take home of Rastafarians, I'll begin there. They are generally the opposite to a true Rastafarian. However, some, often display similar characteristics.

Generally, I found that they have become so used to hustling their fellow rudeboys on the beach for sales, that they have become, on the surface, self-centred and pretty hard faced. Some, cling on to some of the early Rastafari philosophy from the original Nyabinghi tribe, who stood up against the white political movements in Jamaica, born from the hostility with the early European settlers.

Of course everywhere we go we experience people who may not take a liking to us, and no more so is that true than in Scotland from the skinheads, or NEDs, being Non-Educated Delinquents, as they are so un-flatteringly termed. Which, in their defence, is wrong and uncalled for. EVERYONE has a story. Everyone has a reason for being in the quality of life they appear to be in, whether positive or negative and everyone else around us reflects certain truths of ourselves: good and bad, no matter where or how they are brought up.

My story isn't about what colour you are, or about racism; but the little I will say about it is: the people of the Caribbean have more of a reason to be racist than we Europeans do; yet in my experience in Scotland, more so than England, is that we are much more racist. It usually gets better as we get older and wiser, but many unfortunately just get older.

What is the difference of forgiving a fake Rasta Rudeboy who knows no better, and a Scottish (skin')NED (Non-educated-delinquent)? Who equally has just been listening to his unaware elders and reflecting on an unsatisfied life in his violent verbal behaviour, of which it usually only is.

It is a shame that we are not taught at school that our thoughts define us and have an effect on the quality of our lives. That even if we do not act on the thought, that those thoughts may, through subsequent speech, lead to another human being acting upon them; and therefore creating some of that subsequent action to be linked back to the original thinker.

This is similar to how karma works. You don't have to be Indian or believe in religion or Indian philosophy to respect this train of thought. Action, karma, through lifeforce, known as Chi in China or Prana in India, make up our subjective mind; and the source of thought may be described similarly to the chicken and egg paradox.

One needs the other, but how do you determine what came first? According to evolutionary biology the egg came first, as in single-celled creatures from which the egg-laying chicken evolved, but that doesn't explain how the single-celled creatures came to be. This is a little too deep and heavy at this stage, so I will continue telling the story.

There are two other Rastafarian tribes making three in total, the Nyabinghi we looked at briefly above, the Twelve Tribes of Israel and the Bo Bo Dreads.

My now ex-girlfriend, who was still holding out for me at the time, arrived a month or two later than I did and for a while things were a little more settled in terms of alcohol and substance abuse, as I was officially not drinking under her eyes anyway. I would take cocaine without her knowing, or so I thought, when we were out with friends though.

At the New Years party we went to, some white surfer guy, an Architect I think, noticed the signs and tried looking up my nose for proof. It was pretty obvious that night but my girlfriend never asked me about it. She tried finding work as a nurse but with us not being married was unsuccessful as she needed a work visa.

So my girlfriend took longer to settle and was bored during the day. We spent our weekends like she spent her week days, at the beach, although at the start we went sightseeing quite a lot. When I reflect back now I can see that I was selfish moving us there, it may have been different if we were married and she could work.

I honestly don't think we were intimate the whole time she was there. Christmas was quite nice, spent having what could have been a romantic meal in a hotel nearby, and for her birthday the following March I took her to a nice hotel for the weekend. Still she didn't cheer up nor show any desire to be with me. She didn't like the house we lived in, despite it being a three bedroom masonry house, with a nice garden, hosting coconut palm trees, a mango tree and some other little trees and shrubs with a big lawn that surrounded the house.

It was a nice area where the most expensive hotel, Sandy Lane was sited nearby. She would see famous people on the beach and chat to the press photographer who I befriended, having been in that profession a little earlier in my life. I actually asked him how I could go about getting a job like his, but he said I would have to start in London.

In the April she left to go back home to her parents who lived in Cheshire. This had been another good reason for previously moving to Chester from London. She got work as a bank nurse which is temporary work with very good hourly rates, and she would call me, and I her, daily, she would tell me she was feeling horny, but all that did was make me remember all of the times I suspected her with a doctor. She used to have a thing for the doctors before we started going out and I knew things hadn't miraculously changed.

For a few months I maintained sobriety without even a sneaky one, the longest ever for me, since before I was fifteen years old; and then I met Dan who was over from the States doing a one year placement at the university. He was studying psychology and philosophy and was a really interesting guy. I had started sailing on Saturday afternoons with an accountant from work who had a yacht. I first met a Scottish girl, who became a good friend, then Dan joined the crew one day and we became good friends too. The day we met we had a few bottles of beer at the beech bar near the club, The Boathouse, after sailing. It was my first drink for months and it felt amazing.

I only had four beers and drove home, feeling okay. The following weekend Dan started chatting to a pretty Dutch girl, Victoria, who was doing a one year work placement as part of her degree. He tried hard to date her but she had a boyfriend back home and was in to none of it. One evening I drove her home from our house and Dan stayed in the house with my girlfriend. I was smoking far too much weed and getting paranoid. He was a good looking, charming man and she didn't want a physical relationship with me, which made me think that she must be frustrated as I was.

Now maybe there was something in the air that I picked up on when I arrived back in the house, or maybe I was just plain paranoid android jealous, but it stayed in my head for weeks, a feeling of doubt and uncertainty. I bottled it up because I liked him a lot as a friend and I loved my girlfriend and did not want to dwell on uncertainty.

Eventually I spoke to him about it after she had left and he denied it, saying he didn't fancy her. I believed him and then to confirm it I spoke to her about it too. It was difficult to say, she was very good at hiding her feelings but I took their word for it.

Another experience similar to this that I bottled up that equally had some part in things to follow was my Rasta friend from work. He had asked to stay in my house one afternoon to finish watching a football game. We had been smoking as usual at lunch time and my girlfriend, looking sexy as usual in her bikini, was home, which was unusual because she was usually at the beach. He loved football, I never have got the game, so I just thought at the time he really did want to watch it and so I was cool with him staying back. You see my girlfriend could go back to the beach and he could just lock the gate on his way out, by just snapping the padlock on the veranda, which in my mind at the time was what would happen.

At the time I thought nothing of it, but then, days later it started to niggle at me. I asked him some months later when she had left and he said he was surprised that I hadn't minded him staying when he asked, which just made me think and worry about it even more, despite him denying anything had happened.

At this stage I had finished with my girlfriend over the phone, following a month or two after she left. This came about because I cheated on her, having been unable to contain my frustration after she left. It happened with a French girl I met on a weekend sailing to the island of Bequia.

The one hundred mile journey to Bequia from Barbados by boat was a direct one, the prevailing wind generally goes from east to west off the Atlantic. Bequia, being the northern little isle of the Grenadines, just south of St Vincent, is west of Barbados.

We travelled through the night. The skipper was getting on a bit in age. He was a really nice gentlemen, but his safety awareness was nil. There were no life jackets aboard and despite the huge swells in the middle of the ocean fifty miles from any coast, the crew was accessing the deck with no safety ropes.

The stern or rear of the yacht, where the external cockpit is, would rise up with each wave as we surfed along, until the wave overtook us and then the bow, the front of the vessel would roll up until another wave came along. The boat was coasting along too fast as the wind and swell rose up as the night went on, the mainsail, being the largest sail at the rear, was reefed before we left port which meant that the sail was not fully hoisted and should provide more control in high winds.

However, the sail was still capturing too much wind power and we needed to take it down. Also, the flat out run in the dark and the swell of the rising waves gave risk to the boat gybing, where the boom, the horizontal section of aluminium or wood that the sail attaches to, moves violently across the cockpit with the risk of knocking someone out. So as forecrew I went up on deck to drop the mainsail and then erect the jib, which is a triangular sail at the front of the boat. It requires the sail to be connected to a rope, the Jib stay, and then hoisted to the top of the mast. The sail is then controlled by the jib sheets, which are ropes connected to the ends of the sail and extended into the cockpit.

The helmsman can then control which side of the boat the sail is on to affectively catch the wind. The jib is easier to control in high winds on a run with the wind coming from behind the boat.

The boat was rolling so hard in four directions with waves violently bashing into the hull and rocking it forwards and backwards and my bare feet would leave the deck at times. It was important to always have a hold of something like the mast or the stays, being the wires that support the mast. It was a cloudy, moonless night with little visibility, except what came from the mast light above. This made it even more difficult to balance and see what was available to hold onto.

With one hand I started to unwind the rope on the mast that held the mainsail up and my other arm was wrapped around the mast, holding on for my life. All it would take was one bounce of the boat in the tidal, swelling gale and I would be overboard with no life jacket and the boat whizzing along so fast I would be half a mile behind, lost in the dark ocean, before they had chance to react and turn the boat around. Even if they did turn the boat in time to find me, with the noise of the gale and the wind in the sails, shouting would not be of much use to locate me either.

With that in mind I carefully picked my point within the semi cycle of lurching to let go of the mast and give me two hands to undo the final tie, to allow the mainsail to come down. Following another short break of holding on to the mast I then pulled the jib up the mast by holding onto the rope with both hands firmly and using the tightness to keep my balance, heaving as hard as I could, I got the sail up fast, enabling me to grab the mast again with my right arm, wrapping it around and then tie of the rope so that the sail stayed up.

Having changed the sails I carefully made my way back to the cockpit and we continued at a slightly safer pace. There were four of us and we took turns to keep watch throughout the night, with two going below for a sleep and two staying in the cockpit, usually for two-hour shifts. The boat was steered by a tiller, a length of wood that is attached to the rudder via a spindle. There was no autopilot as the yacht was very basic. We had to constantly make small adjustments for the waves and wind hitting the boat.

It felt like having a hangover when we arrived, but we were on a buzz. The sun was up and we dropped the anchor in the bay and made it to shore in the dingy. We chilled in the apartment for a couple of hours and tried to get some sleep before the race meeting around midday and a race following that.

That night we were tired and most went to bed, but this was when I met the French girl and my sexual frustration kept me out longer. Her race crew finally talked me into having a drink although I had tried explaining that I wasn't a drinker. It had been a while since the beer with Dan, but I took the excuse and had a few. The first night I had some tolerance. I did end up kissing the girl though, but didn't get too drunk. The next night I scored some weed from a local and because I was stoned, I got really drunk, fell in the door in the early hours and woke my fellow crew up. Obviously they weren't too happy.

One of the guys who was anti-drugs and didn't drink, told our skipper I had bought some weed. Luckily, the skipper was pretty cool and didn't tell my boss when we got back. Remember, he was the company accountant.

The best part of this trip to Bequia though, was the return crossing to Barbados. We set off on Sunday evening after the skipper asked me if I was taking grass back. I told him not to worry, I had given the rest of it away. He was worried the dogs back in Barbados port would sniff it out and get him in trouble. The sail back was expected to take at least twice as long so we didn't expect to arrive until the same time the following day. We had plenty of water and enough food for twenty four hours, as you don't eat much when you are sailing, you're either on shift and steering the boat or else you want to sleep.

The reason for the long return is that you couldn't usually sail directly to Barbados because that is the direction that the prevailing wind comes from. A sailing boat must sail with the wind or at an angle to the wind, approximately forty five degrees off it. The technical term is a close haul, also sometimes known as being on a beat, as in trying to beat the wind.

I forgot to mention that navigation is obviously very important when out at sea because you have no landmarks to recognise where you are. The modern way is via satellite navigation and so every two hours, when changing shift, we would record our global co-ordinates with the small satellite navigation device and then plot the X, Y co-ordinates on a nautical chart. This allowed us to know how far we were travelling, at what speed and more importantly, when to change direction. Too far off course and you could spend a lot longer at sea than required.

That first night we made excellent headway. When the dawn broke, but before the sun rose properly, I was on shift and steering the boat. I let a fellow crew mate go to sleep on the bench in the cockpit and the skipper and other crew were sleeping below. There had been a nice steady wind and the swell was not too bad so there was no danger and no need for my buddy on the bench to stay awake.

In the dawn twilight I noticed ripples of water moving around me and heard a distinctive noise like fish jumping out of the water. At first I wondered if it was a school of flying fish, but usually they pass very quickly, chasing whatever it is they are trying to eat; but this noise went on for about twenty minutes.

As the light got better I noticed that we were being accompanied by dolphins. Beautiful, intelligent looking creatures they were. I had let everyone keep sleeping because I was enjoying the sober tranquility of the moment. It was amazing and the dolphins just topped it off. Eventually I shook my crew mate awake and he woke the others so that they could see them too.

The dolphins accompanied us for another half hour or so, and when they left it seemed that they took the wind with them. We had lots of fuel stashed under the cockpit benches, enough to get back to Barbados, so we weren't worried at first about the wind disappearing. It is the hot Caribbean and calmness can be expected, of course.

After cruising along for around an hour the engine just stopped. Our skipper knew straight away that there was a problem because he knew the fuel tank would still be at least three quarters full. He tried what he knew to get it to work again but it was dead, something serious. It turned out later to be a fault with the drive shaft and so it never would have been repairable at sea.

We were like a sitting duck with no feet for paddles. We bobbed around in the swell of the ocean for about two hours and the sun rose higher and higher and we got hotter and hotter. The skipper started to worry and talked of the possibility of having to call the coast guard if the wind didn't return before the day was out.

He had plotted our position and we were approximately half way, some fifty miles off Bequia and the same from Barbados, the nearest lands to our position. We were drifting off course with the steady tidal swells and this was a concern, as was the lack of food and water. We started rationing the water intake and decided not to eat anything else after a breakfast of dry crackers.

Another two hours passed and still no sign of wind yet, not even a breeze, the sails just flapped ideally with the swell rocking the boat gently from side to side.

Then an idea came to me, we had a blown up rubber dingy tied down to the front of our yacht deck and we had a small two stroke engine for it which was down below in the cabin. If we could get the dingy to pull or push us along then it might just get us to some wind. Skipper agreed that it was worth a try and we unleashed the rubber dingy and lowered it overboard.

I climbed down into the dingy and they lowered the outboard down by rope. We kept it tied on whilst I fixed it to the dingy transom. The swell wasn't big but enough to make me nervous of letting go of the engine until it was clamped on. I had tied the front and the rear of the dingy to the side of the yacht next to the cockpit at the rear. Then I tied the engine off too, so that it stayed in the middle position, pointing forwards, and I started it up. To our good fortune it wasn't long before the yacht picked up speed and was moving steadily toward our new compass heading.

However, we must have only have been moving between two and three miles per hour because when we checked our position before nightfall, we had only covered ten miles and were still forty miles from Barbados. There was still no sign of any wind and so we took shifts again. The engine would run out of fuel every two hours and that was when we swapped. I think the crew had recognised my confidence in the situation and requested that I fill up the engine, it was quite difficult to keep my balance in the dingy with the night swell raising the dingy up and down.

Someone would shine a torch at the engine whilst I wedged my knees into the rear corners of the dingy, kneeling down to try and keep in the boat. With the dingy bouncing around in the dark it made it really hard to fill up the tank but at least the boat wasn't flying along and there was no fear of me being lost at sea if I bounced out of the dingy.

We travelled like this all night, filling up at least five times, when someone noticed the faint lights of Barbados in the distance; it was probably fifteen to twenty miles off.

Our hopes raised considerably and it was only shortly afterwards that the wind picked up and we hoisted the mainsail. We kept the little engine going anyway and when we got into port around five or six am, we used it to help us steer into port. I sat in the dingy and controlled the engine, putting it into reverse when required, whilst the Skipper steered the yacht with the tiller as we had been doing all night.

This was the longest I had been at sea, although I love boats and it was only for thirty six hours, when I set foot on the concrete jetty I was relieved to be off the boat. I was also dizzy, it felt like the concrete key under my feet was moving. I was also really hungry. My friend and I drove straight to the bagel cafe in Sunsetcrest before I dropped her home. This would have been a good time to take a break from the cocaine, having been off it for a weekend.

Loneliness kicked in deep in the weeks to follow though. It is always best, I think, to have events to look forward to, such as a holiday, and now that my little sailing holiday was done I had a long time to wait until I was off next. I had booked two weeks in July to go home and see my family and friends in the UK.

Rather naughtily the company had picked the American holiday allowance and yet paid comparative to UK wages, thereby short-changing you by approximately one week's holiday and paying you relative to UK wages. Meaning you were almost working a week for free, whereas in the US, wages tend to be higher to accommodate their working ethic of less annual holidays.

My Rasta friend had a daughter and another one on the way when I met him. His youngest was now born, and apart from our ganja lunches we hung about less and less. I did however, start hanging out a lot with his old school mates who were both single.

We went out at least once a week, clubbing. They didn't do coke. I was just in a habit of doing it myself and although they knew I liked it now and then, I kept it to myself for a couple of reasons. One, I didn't want to be responsible for getting them on it, and two, I didn't want them worrying about me. They usually never knew when I was on it, I had become used to the strength and knew how much to take before getting off my head, so as to be confidant and in control.

When we weren't out they were usually at my house watching the pirate cable TV I had got installed, or I was out on my own drinking, taking charlie and meeting new people. One such person was a lassie from Scotland. She was staying with her Auntie and we met on a Sunday in a bar in Holetown that had become my regular Sunday haunt. I loved a good drink on a Sunday, and this part of town was a walk from my house and just so happened to be the place to hang out on a Sunday night. The rest of the week it was fairly quiet, but on a Sunday the party would be outside, with the main street lined with a mix of holiday-makers and locals, drinking and dancing together.

Out of the blue I got an unexpected email from my old friend in London, who says he is coming on holiday in a couple of weeks with his girlfriend.

As luck would have it, I had great, pure tasting coke every week. Then the week before he came I couldn't get any from my usual guys, so I went through someone new and it was disappointing, the hit was there but not as quick; it crept up gradually too, probably because it took more to get high, and then it's too late once it's in your system, and all of a sudden you were quite a bit more higher than you previously realised. Ironically, when I went home, his brother would provide me with three grams of the exact same gritty cut stuff in London, maybe it was even the same batch from the Caribbean, or possibly just a known way of cutting it.

His brother had said at the time that it was meant to be better than normal gear and afterwards, when I tried it, I wished I had just bought the normal stuff. We were both probably mislead in an attempt for it to be sold off. We even paid slightly more for it, idiots!

When my mate arrived I showed him the nightlife. I knew his girlfriend quite well too. He used to live at his girlfriends Mum's before I left London, and was still staying there.

The club was pretty tight on drugs and the toilets were checked regularly, so you had to be quite careful. Silently as possible taking a quick dip and snort off the corner of a credit card and forget racking lines up. Sometimes a bouncer would be at the door listening. You had to be always ready to drop and flush and keep your back to the unlocked door, your ears alert and your reactions ready. With that, I gave them some of their own gear and warned them about security, so as to avoid going in together and attracting attention.

That night we met two local sisters, both born in Barbados, but now living in England and just over on holiday visiting family. When my pal left at the end of the week, I continued seeing one of the sisters as they were staying for another week. I introduced the usual suspects to them one night and they brought their other sister out.

That night my Rasta mate pulled Scottish lassie in my house and later told his wife. Some weeks later, I felt really bad about my part in it because he had two girls and his wife was lovely too, she had been very welcoming and kind to me. It's not that I had a part in it as such but it happened in my house and that made me feel guilty around his wife, especially as I had introduced them.

It was some days later, the night before my new Bajan friend was due to go home to England, that she stayed the night. Having spent a lot of time with her, smoking and just hanging out, I was beginning to think she had just become another friend like the other girls I had been hanging out with. Out of all the girls I fancied at that time, she was the most appealing. I had been with a couple of local Bajan girls, but not of her beauty, nor shared interests, and I think we really clicked too.

After she left I missed her a lot. I never really called home much, but in the month to follow I called the UK at least three times to speak to her.

A few friends from work would go out most Fridays. One of my buddies had still been trying to score with one of the sisters who lived in Barbados and one night I was out with them both partying. He was tired and said he was going home. She said she wanted to stay and I said I'd drop her home as was on my way. At the time, high on coke and just dancing in my own world, I was unaware of the possible consequences, but obviously my mate wasn't.

He called me the following morning to enquire if she stayed at mine and I denied anything happened, although it had. It wasn't for fear of fighting him that I denied the fact we got together, but for fear of hurting him emotionally and I valued his company and friendship.

I felt awful, because I hadn't meant it to happen. I really liked her sister still back in the UK, but she was annoyed with me, having heard that I was bragging having slept with her. Which wasn't the case, I had just agreed how lovely she was and that we had been hanging out. The guy who told her this was someone I met in the strip club, who coincidentally, knew her from England.

He probably fancied her and wanted to use me to make himself look better; I noticed he never explained where he met me!

My feelings of empty loneliness were now being replaced with complicated relationships, including falling for the sister of the girl I had been having strong feelings for, who was also fancied by my mate.

Then one day one of my boys drops by my house with a girl from Trinidad who he had met on the beach, but had expressed her interest in meeting a white guy. Being cool as he is, he didn't mind she wasn't into him and helped her out!

So now I have this beautiful Trinidadian girl at my house and flirting with me, my pal just leaves and asks if I'll drop her back at the uni later where she is living in student accommodation. So what is there to do but go and have a few beers and get to know each other? You can imagine what happened next.

Now, despite not being in an actual relationship, two girls are forming the opinion that we are. Complications had only begun up to this point, now the comings and goings were starting to trip me up. I had befriended two girls at the end of my road too, who worked in shops next door to each other. Neither girls knew I was interested in the other. An American girl dropped by my house one day unexpected, after I had chatted her up on my regular Sunday-nighter in Holetown. She was an Archeologist and I had forgot that I had given her my address. Although she had played hard to get she knocked on my door sober and near enough jumped on me as soon as she came in. She was heading home the next day fortunately.

It would be hard to believe things could get much more complicated, but then, for some crazy reason I cannot comprehend, I let a beach bum girl, who I had my suspicions was a prostitute, befriend me, and move in! She cleaned my house everyday for food and a room. I tried it on with her a couple of times after coming in off my face, but she would have none of it. Then one night she is out with me, drinking, when I ask her again.

She says that she would like to watch me have sex with someone else. So knowing a girl, my first local girl one night stand, I called her on the way home and she obliged. Although, when we got back I didn't feel like an audience and so we just went to our own rooms. The next night I went out again with my lodger, and this time she wanted more than to just watch and here another addition to my complicated life occurred, which was bound to end in stress and pain at some point.

I never found out for sure, but after that night I was even more sure that she was a prostitute, she knew what she was about - a mind blowing experience is all I will say. The message I am trying to get across is not that I was a dirty slag bag but that I was weaving a web of deceit and confusion that had a heavy price yet to pay. Though dirty slag bag is true, and it didn't feel good to be acting like one.

There is only so much a mind that is usually responsible can take. When drunk and high with not a care, the world was my oyster you might say; when sober the reality was very different. I did care and I did feel regret and I was thoroughly ashamed of my behaviour.

Still, it was the yearly carnival now and no time to stop for regrets. The partying up to now had been tame compared to what was to come. For a month solid, maybe two, it was every night just about, and all weekend. The days became nights and the nights days, and work was done in autopilot with eyes half closed. Sometimes work came around too soon and sick days were called, or worse, I went in still in a different world.

Responsibility for my actions had gone with my self-respect. When you lose self respect you are in a bad way, for you can't respect others unless you respect yourself. This goes the same for trust. When you drop to this level you won't be aware of it at the time usually, but please know that if you do recognise it, that you are in a really bad place. Danger lurks at every corner for the person without a care.

Trouble started around this time in all sorts of ways. One night I caught my thumb in the car door. Having parked at the club whilst high and having a bit of obsessive compulsive disorder I thought I'd left my lighter in the car, my hand followed my semi-conscious thought and wham, crack, "Ow!"

That same night I met a beautiful girl, who with the flowing cocaine, helps me forget the pain. With the chase in mind I have no fear. I stay longer than I should and on my way home alone after too many rums I feel I need some more gear. The sun is up when I drop by my weed dealer, an old Rastafarian. I usually wouldn't ask a Rasta for coke, it's not their way, but he knows everyone and once helped me before. He thinks I have things in control; how wrong he was for believing in my false confidence.

Still, the only fault was mine, and having scored the biggest bag of coke you could hope for, I wondered why I didn't come to him more for this, instead of the rudeboys. Of course, he had to go get it from the rude boys, but because they thought this elder was selling-on, they gave him a pure uncut bag at a no profit price. I was used to maybe a tenth of this amount for the same price, but I knew that was safer, I was aware of my addiction now. My nose was starting to burn away from the inside, the piece of thin membranous skin between the nostrils was getting thinner and I'm sure the actual thicker skin that's visible at the bottom of the nose the nasal septum, was also slowly disappearing.

A ritual before bed routine had commenced, including me drawing up water into my nostrils and blowing it out, to try and wash the chemical remains away in an attempt to slow down the process of skin cell killing that was going on so regularly; at least three times a week on average and nearly every day over the carnival.

After scoring my big bag deal I went home to hide it, and then, after a line, I took a little in my pocket, went to the shop, bought a quarter bottle of Hennessey brandy and went to pretend that I was staying in the Sandy Lane hotel where all the famous stars go. I would only do this on occasion for a treat because the hotel security staff were quite sharp on picking up that I was a local now.

Incidentally, I had noticed my lodger on this beach previously, doing yoga and handstands and, like me probably, on the prowl for a rich partner. I had remembered seeing her when I was with my girlfriend. It was hard to forget her amazing athletic body and the tantric yoga-like poses she so masterfully was good at.

That morning on the beach after a couple of lines of Charlie in the posh Sandy Lane toilets a beach bum I knew quite well walked past the beach and for some reason I decided to go a walk with him. He told me he had been living in the mountains on the east coast to get off crack and wouldn't do it again, I think he could tell I was high and was himself in danger of wanting some. We ended up going for a drive, drank the brandy and met a blind date I had been set up with and so far had delayed meeting up with.

That didn't go great and after a day of beach bumming around and skiving of work we ended up clubbing, then eventually back to my house for a smoke. The guy ended up asking me for some charlie to put in his joint after all and in the morning he asked me if he could borrow my car. Hung over from two days and nights partying I just murmoured 'Aye'.

I got up eventually around midday, it was a Saturday. No sign of my beach bum mate nor my car and having thought I dreamt lending him it, the hard reality kicked in. I thought to myself:

'Where the fuck is my car? Is he coming back?'.

Around six o'clock I get a call from the police.

My car has been impounded after my so called mate, who by the way turns out had no license, has smashed it up high on crack.

'Shit' I think,

'I've gone and got him back on the gear just by having him hang around me'.

It doesn't take much for a relapse especially on an island where drugs are never far away. The car was a company one and this was a serious issue, no license meant no insurance.

Between the partying I did try and keep healthy, I enjoyed surfing and would very occasionally join a mate for a dip before work. I had bought a surf board, but like the Rudeboy I was becoming, I had not bothered with lessons and would head out into the big Atlantic surf, often after a joint, and get washed up in six foot plus waves. I was mad already, just awaiting an official stamp, of course.

Boogie boarding I had mastered, where you strap on flippers or fins and use them to get enough speed to catch a wave on a body board. This provided endless fun and I would brave any wave, just about.

How I didn't get myself killed on the surf board I'll never know. I also ran and exercised on the beach to keep muscle tone. Of course, this was just for vanity purposes to attract the ladies and not to necessarily keep healthy.

'Open your eyes and look within' - Bob Marley Exodus, 1976 in reply to Jamacia elections, the year he was shot at and chased off his own island home.

7 BLACK MAGIC

After the beach in the evening I would sometimes grab a real coffee from the cafe at the end of my road. There were often two guys sat outside the cafe. Rumour had it the older guy, George was gay, not that it has anything to do with the story other than, I wonder now if that was why he was trying to befriend me.

Although at the time, it was the younger guy who I felt was trying to lure me into something. I didn't feel this properly until one evening after I'd invited the guys over for a drink, they turned up at my door and so joined my mates and I for a smoke. The younger guy made a comment like 'give me a month and he'll be one of us'; or 'give me a month and we'll have him', or something to that effect.

With the weed making me paranoid, those words rattled around my head for days and I believe opened doors in my mind that really were safer left alone.

Following the right off of my car and subsequent stress, together with the fact my body and mind was showing signs of deterioration, such as pains in my sides following heavy nights and a visible increase in the size of veins below my waist, that usually went down the following morning.

The heart palpations had not begun yet, but a shortness of breath, not asthmatically but heart related.

The palpitations were present now and then when I was very high, just when my breath reached the limit of the in-breath, it would become too painful to breathe in anymore. I knew this for the sign that it was; my circulation was suffering, I was losing weight too and struggling to look after myself at home. I was too erratic to food-shop properly or cook.

It was around this period that I tried to kick the coke into touch, one night after either palpations, nose sensitivity, vein bulging, pains in sides or all symptoms occurring.

One night I flushed a substantial amount of cocaine down the toilet, thinking that this would prevent me from wasting money on it again. However, no such luck. The next time I was out on the town, drinking, I bought it again half cut.

The thing about alcohol and my history is that I never would have tried drugs had I not been drunk, with my inhibitions lowered.

Unfortunately, I can't claim to have never been part of the reason for some trying drugs and I am ashamed of the part I've played. I've wondered since if life would be different for myself and those unfortunate souls. Also I've wondered what life struggles they have gone through, some I know still depend on weed to get through their day and deal with the stressful lives they have created.

It would have been an idea to take public transport, making it harder for me to go and find drugs, but it wasn't illegal to drive having consumed alcohol, although if you did crash there were complications with insurance, if caught. Believe it or not this helped me control my drink addiction, meaning that I didn't make a complete idiot of myself and maybe saved me getting shot, for I remained sober enough to drive home. However, this is obviously highly inadvisable, as hurting or killing someone from unawareness is unacceptable and will be on your conscience for life.

I leant on the drugs far too much for a higher high and got used to it as the norm. That's another problem with illegal drugs, once experienced, the legal drug, alcohol, is not as affective at getting you high anymore and the brain seeks the highest highs. This fact that your brain seeks highness and happiness actually helps the addict to get on the straight and narrow, as will be explained later.

Having realised that my alcohol use was still a problem and that although it was almost contained via my use of illicit drugs, it was also the source of my drug addiction. I sought to deal with the problem from source and try and stop drinking again.

So one Saturday, after a quiet night in, smoking weed and watching films from the movie rental shop, I went to a book shop and that's when I bought Susan Powter's book on Alcoholism: Sober and Staying that Way.

I read a lot that day and it made sense. My biochemistry in regard to alcohol consumption must be different to normal folk. I had an in-balance and believed that something biologically was wrong with how I processed alcohol. The book advised to stop taking so much sugar, as that is what alcohol is mainly made of.

By avoiding sugar, you help starve the cravings. It also prescribed various vitamins to re-nourish the body, including vitamin B which is usually deficient in alcoholics.

This kind of remedy is good for the mind too, you are used to self-medicating and so to try and fix the problem with pills is easier to start than you think. It gives you something to focus on and believe in too. I would add, long as the pills are just vitamins!

To successfully stop drinking it takes a holistic approach, you need nourishment, good food, not crap, so white flour is out too. Beans, pulses, wholegrain rice and breads are good. Not too much yeasty food though. Diet is very important to begin with, even just giving up sugar is easier than giving up alcohol.

People often ask me how did you maintain being a vegetarian? Well it was much easier than not drinking alcohol! And yes, ladies and gentlemen, that is a major reason why I stopped eating meat. I did want to do it for the animals and for the same conscious reasons Indian Yogis and Rastafarians give it up for, but let me be frank, if you don't give things up for your own reasons then you run a risk of going back to whatever it was you used to do.

Just to reiterate then, to assist in giving something up that you really do not want to, try giving something else up, preferably at the same time and something that will, hopefully, assist in giving up the main thing that it is you need to give up.

To assist further, try not to look at it as giving something up, but gaining something. If I stop eating sugar, I'll gain my athletic body back and be thin. If I give up drinking alcohol, I will control my drug addiction and stay away from the dealer, or my sex addition or whatever it is you need to stop doing.

Again, don't think of it as giving something up, try and replace it. So if you stop drinking for health, go to the gym and get fit. Focus on the gym.

The addictive mind works in the background like our phone aps do these days. We get constant reminders that we need software updates and the like. We need to sometimes take control of these automatic messages and put a stop to them because we need our RAM for something more important.

If we need to get home without stopping to buy drugs, we do this by avoiding the pub, and we do this by avoiding the sugar hit after lunch and the caffeine when tired.

Coffee was another thing strongly advised to avoid, for it works like cocaine. Caffeine addiction is similar to crack, didn't you know? Well any alcoholic I know, if I'm being honest with you, would describe their highs like a crack head would his, and also would probably confess to be willing to try illicit drugs, if off their head, drunk, or if they were unable, for whatever reason, to consume alcohol.

So if caffeine is no good for the crack addict, it's no good for the alcoholic either. When you hear this it sounds so simple doesn't it? We are what we eat and drink, yes? We can balance our bodies with a balanced diet and be healthy, or we can take a lot of one type of thing and become unhealthy and addictive to it, in all its forms.

So firstly, no sugar.

Secondly, no white flour. Eat only wholegrain before the goodness within the grain is ground down to dust, which is what white flour is, the dust without the goodness.

Thirdly, check the food packaging for added sugar and other unwanted chemicals.

Finally, take regular multi-vitamins. Including vitamin B

Add the above to regular exercise and filling in the rest of your spare time that you have from not drinking with something enjoyable: For example, treat yourself to something you like doing that you would have spent the money on by wasting it on booze and drugs.

This is very important if you want to be successful. Try not to make it weed, or other intoxicants that you replace alcohol with.

Trust me - playing one drug off against another does not work. In-fact, try not to replace the consumption with another consumption full stop, use the free time to fulfil long lost desires.

Be careful with other potential addictions, like gambling, sex, etc, for they will inevitably lead you back to alcohol once that particular addiction reaches its limit of satisfaction or creates stress for the user, from loss of money, etc.

8 SHIATSU

Had I become aware a little earlier of how serious my predicament was, and really sought the courage and strength to stand up against my addictions, I may have prevented the events that followed.

However, the reality is that sometimes it takes a near-death experience to wake us up. On the way back from the book shop that Saturday, death was obviously on my mind, not consciously, but subconsciously, for I drove past a church slowly, in traffic, and noticed distinctly that a funeral was commencing, from all of the people entering the church dressed in black. For some strange reason this seemed meaningful.

The following week I was a passenger in my Rasta mates car coming back from his house one lunchtime with a joint or two inside us, when I tell him the experience. As I finish my short story he points out of his window, slows the car a little and says:

'hey Steve, check this out'.

It's only another funeral, with people in black going into the church, and a hearse outside. Both times the funeral was to my right-hand side, within a week of each other, and both gave me a spooky meant to be feeling. That weekend I tried to stay in, but I was bored, lonely, and being led by desire to go out and find a girl. I didn't really need an excuse, but some company would be nice, so I go for a few beers, but like normal, I cannot stay away from the coke and before I know it I'm heading down the gap, in St Lawrence, to score a bit.

At least this time it was just a bit, and although I had some left the next day, I flushed it down the toilet and attempted another week with none. Usually I went out Sunday, as mentioned, and finished off any coke I had. Also, I was likely to go out mid-week, maybe Wednesday, have a rest Thursday then hit it all weekend.

This particular week I decided to take a friend's offer up on a free Shiatzu massage. I really was trying to straighten myself out in my own way. She obliged and it felt great. I had been suffering from very tense shoulders and neck and sometimes was restricted in movements there, a common thing for people burning the candle at both ends, unaware that the nights out are not relaxing the body, but putting more stress on the nervous system and making it harder to deal with everyday work and life pressures.

I had started some deep breathing exercises that I had learnt from her Shiatzu book on our sailing trip in Bequia. I asked her if it was okay to do this during the massage and she said yes. The massage itself wasn't like a normal massage, much of the time her hands were not even touching my skin. I thought I could feel the stress loosening and the energy flowing, less blocked.

With the added breathing and visualisation, it was an amazing experience. I'd like to add that I had chosen to stay sober and free from the influence of weed, although I'm likely to have smoked earlier in the day, my mind was clear enough.

9 GHOST WRITING

I sat at my dining table one evening, like most evenings alone, when not out partying; just sitting drinking coffee, surfing the internet and smoking weed. I tried not to keep drink in the house. Whenever I had a bottle of rum, I couldn't keep it for long before necking it alone. It felt safer to smoke alone, than drink alone.

I've mentioned already the interest of two strange men from the café at the end of the street, who appeared friendly, but mysterious, and have mentioned some strange things hinting toward the practise of black magic. It had unnerved me, especially as I knew nothing about them, where they lived, or what their intentions were. Sometimes I would feel that I was not alone, that I was being watched, or that someone was outside. I remember having joined a Rastafarian forum website where the founder called himself the Conquering Lion of Judah.

At some point, I took up this name also, and would sign off emails as AKA (also known as) *The Lion of Judah*. It was a bit of fun, but a part of me was connected to this changing aspect of myself. One of the other names I came up with for myself during this period of what we now term as blogging, was *Green Tea Buoy*.

I had been drinking green tea and associated the healing properties with something spiritual. The word Buoy symbolised mankind, as a representation of all girls and boys, bobbing about in the sea having broken our anchors. In my imagination the buoys would eventually merge together and become one.

So, after posting a section regarding my thoughts on life, etc, on the Rasta site, I rolled myself another joint and pondered what I had written. There was a white envelope on the table and whilst seemingly thinking of nothing in particular I took up a pen in my hand and dotted the paper with my eyes closed. I continued to do a series of dot to dots, in a small area of the envelope. When I looked at what I had drawn, I was amazed to see the distinctive shape of a dragon, or maybe a Scottish Lion, stood upright, as per the flag of Scotland, although the face looked more dragon like.

Then for reasons unknown, probably nothing other than staring blankly ahead, deep in contemplation, my attention to the detail of a large painting on the wall became intensified. I could not stop looking at it, I took in the painter's vision as if I were the painter. I imagined drawing the rowing boat that sat to the side of a beach house. Both objects were the main feature of the picture, together with a large palm tree, all in the foreground with the beach behind and around, and the sea and sky as the backdrop.

Then once I had examined every detail of the picture, my focus widened slightly to take into focus the stereo speaker to the left of the picture, that was sat on a small table with the 90's mini-Hi-fi stereo in the middle and another speaker to the side of it.

The rectangular speaker unit was a standard one, having a large black circular speaker to the bottom of the unit with a smaller circular black speaker above it. The smaller circle was within a triangle of three small circular dots. My attention never left the picture whilst taking in the detail of the speaker unit. A fan was whirring below and to the right of the picture and apart from that there was no other sound.

The smaller circle of the speaker slowly became my main focus of attention and although still able to distinguish the various aspects within the picture, they became blurry. One by one the small circular dots that formed the triangle around the small circular black speaker began to disappear. It didn't matter if I blinked my sight remained focussed on the speaker and the picture and the dots didn't re-appear.

Before I go any further, I do NOT recommend trying this, especially if under the influence of anything mind-altering. It was the start of events that led to me going mad. If you don't reach that chapter before looking into things too deeply under the influence of drugs, take my word that there is no physical pain imaginable that would come close to the mental pain experienced during a full blown psychosis. You watch yourself going mad, trapped in fear that you will never escape. Doomed to live out the rest of your life in a rotating circle, where all thoughts are undirected, out of control and start and end at the same point. Imagine going round and round on a merry-go-round forever, sure that you should be able to get off, but incapable of taking the necessary actions to do so.

When all three dots disappeared, colours briefly appeared as speckles on the surface of the small black speaker, and then the whole speaker unit rose up off the table and moved to the left, over the stereo and hovered above the other speaker. At this point my attention faltered, in fright or awe, at what was happening. I cannot remember at what point I lost sight of the picture, nor if it mattered, but as soon as my attention lapsed, the speaker moved back to its original position on the table.

I did not hear or see signs of wires being pulled, tangled or affected and was quite sure I had just caused the illusion to happen through straining my eyes and that it didn't actually happen. Within moments of the speaker returning, after having maybe half a minute to contemplate and regain normal sight, I looked down the hall toward the bedrooms and there within the full height of the hall was a black shadow. The hall was just to the left of the stereo and directly in front of me, my back was to a large sideboard, the kitchen was directly on my left and the living room on my right.

When pondering the possibility of superstition and whether I am doing the right, moral thing telling this story, i.e. for the right reasons of helping others or enlightening family members or people with similar problems to me, and not for my own benefits; I caught a glimpse of what may be the truth. Too deep to divulge just yet, I need to explain the three Gunas first and Indian Philosophy, but a taster would be to consider a similar theme, the Chinese theory of Yin and Yang.

The symbol of one white and one black comma, joining each other to form a whole, yet blending together from the dark head of Yin to the thin, light tail of Yang and vice-versa.

These symbols, represent the opposite forces and aspects of all things in existence merging in and out of each other like hot and cold, forming a circle of union and wholeness. Each symbol has a small circle of the opposing one within the centre of its main body, symbolising the similarities of the essence, or peak of opposing energies.

For example, the natures of extreme heat and cold energies are to burn. If such a force of darkness exists, it exists as part of a whole and therefore, although frightening in appearance, it's purpose is to not create fear, but actually to cause the end of something, to allow a new, better thing to replace it. Now the shadow that I saw was the shape of what I would imagine the Devil to be, two large horns formed the top of the head, whilst the body included large shoulders and a wide chest area, tailing off to a tapered form; all dark black and distinguishably hovering, just below the ceiling, and just off the floor, against a white-walled background.

Either side of the dark form were two smaller circular forms, flanking the main shadow at its head height. They all just stayed there, no movement towards me thankfully, no voices or sound whatsoever, in fact, I remember a distinct silence. At the time I felt intense fear, as I thought it was the devil, flanked by two dark agents.

After rehab and reflection I realised the two smaller 'ghosts' were exactly as the ones in the film Ghost, where they come for the soul of the bad guy when he dies. The main shape was almost of exact similarity to the big black demon shadow in the Disney film Fantasia.

Both films I saw a few times as a boy. I believe that this experience was the beginning of a message that, amazingly, my subconscious sent to my normal (or abnormal!) everyday consciousness.

The rest of this message quickly unfolds in a way that is beyond everyday understanding. In case you are wondering, I did not take any cocaine that night nor had taken any for a couple of days before. It is extremely uncommon to hallucinate on weed alone, and very rare with cocaine also. I don't think it was a flashback from LSD either, just the state of my impaired nervous system from successive drug and alcohol abuse and sleep deprivation.

10 THREE LITTLE BIRDS

Somehow I managed to get a little sleep the night the shadows appeared, maybe an hour or so, after lying petrified in my bed and all alone with my fear. I woke up at the usual time and got to work at 7.30am on time. My mind was still full of fear, I felt like I was in *The Matrix* film, becoming the *One*. I was constantly contemplating the source of life itself, the origin and nature of God, and after experiencing the shadows, these thoughts intensified beyond normal levels of contemplation; they consumed my every thought.

I sat at my desk as usual. I don't know if the other guys who shared the same office, noticed my change in behaviour, but I didn't fire my laptop up as usual. Instead, I began writing in my works diary. I filled up the pages from that present day to some two or three weeks ahead, the content included one-liners, phrases and words related to what I foresaw as my future. I think my subconscious was at work again, showing me the way, giving me hints that changes were ahead, a journey I could not escape.

I gave my Rasta mate one page that I told him contained important information regarding his future. Then I went in to see my boss and told him I was having problems, not mentioning the shadow experience or the feelings of insight, nor drug use; only that I had a drink problem that was under control when I arrived, but was now totally out of control. I spoke of my intent to temporary leave the island, to go home and seek help and of my wish to return if this was possible.

My boss tried to get me to talk to one of the workers who had gone through similar problems and was now living a sober life, but I was frightened of losing my mind and ending up in a mental hospital. I had heard of people being stuck inside for a long time. Also, during carnival, we passed one, a mental hospital, on the street and everyone in the gardens who had come out to dance to the music looked like they were completely institutionalised, it was frightening to think of being in one of those places.

When my boss knew my mind was made up, he called the head office down the road and spoke to one of the directors. I went down there to see them. One was very religious, the other a reformed alcoholic; they totally understood and were very kind. The religious man was keen to know more of what had made me make such a decision and could probably tell something had happened by my anxiety.

Although it was not my intention to tell them, I ended up explaining what had happened to me the night before. The religious man began praying out loud for me. The offices were not sound-proof and the other people in the office must have wondered what was going on. I can't remember what we discussed regarding when I was to leave, but it wasn't immediately, I think the advice was to check with my boss about any outstanding work to handover and organise for within a week. I remember that was my plan anyway, I didn't want to go and leave unfinished work behind. I was just about finished pricing a supercentre job in Antigua. All I had to do was check through the quantities and prepare a quotation.

I distinctly remember getting in the car at the head office and feeling elated after my meeting with the directors, the prayer had given me a positive feeling, maybe just the care and love shown.

Although it sounds like the cannabis was the cause of my developing problem, I was drinking and taking cocaine between four and six days a week. They would be all night benders, sometimes pulling a sicky to continue drinking on my own. I believe that it takes many aspects to make such a series of events happen, including sleep deprivation, stress and an improper diet. On the other hand some people may only need one of these things to cause such a change in their everyday reality.

I drove straight from my work's head office to my house in Sunset Crest. It would have been late morning. I often went home for a joint at lunch time. On this day, I just wanted to contemplate what I had done and have a smoke before going back to work. As usual I rolled a joint from the tray under the couch with all the stuff on, but instead of sparking it in the living room, I went out the front door onto the enclosed veranda and sat on one of the three white plastic chairs facing outwards towards the front garden.

The rolled joint was in my shirt pocket and I never smoked it. The weather was sunny, despite being the rainy season and it was a nice hot, average Caribbean temperature, probably around 30 degrees Celsius. The patio had iron railings and a gate to my left that I kept locked - it would give me time to flush any drugs down the toilet if the police ever came. Prison in Barbados was worse than the psychiatric hospitals, lots of stories of rape and beatings.

The garden consisted of an expanse of grass with about five trees, a large Mango tree, a couple of coconut and banana trees and a small deciduous tree. The only tree visible from the veranda was the deciduous, to the left, it was more of a big tall shrub really. The front door to the house was to my right and I had my back to the wall of the house, just sitting there looking through the railings.

I must have been sitting their only a few minutes, thinking of nothing in particular, having relaxed with the surroundings; when the bird I had named Frank, after my great uncle, flew over and perched himself on the railings of the gate to my left. Immediately after landing, another bird landed on the railing directly in front of me and then one to the right on the railing too.

Once all three little birds were there, a voice gently entered my head, it was my Uncle Frank's voice. It calmly told me not to delay or hesitate, to leave the island today and not to tell anyone of what had just happened.

Then, as soon as they had come, and in the reverse order, one by one the birds flew away; leaving only Frank, distinguishable by his brown and white markings. He jumped down off the gate railing and landed on the path. He paused and looked right at me, light was emanating from his body and he turned around in a circle, before casually walking down the path and then flying away.

The experience was like no other I had ever felt, it was an intense bliss of unexplainable magnitude. The psychologist Abraham Maslow refers to an experience like this as a 'peak experience'. There are lots of stories of such experiences, usually under similar conditions, where the person is not thinking of anything in particular and almost in a kind of meditative state.

11 VOICES

Before this event with the three little birds, I had never experienced voices in my head before, apart from two brief experiences on LSD mentioned previously. Suddenly, after the birds left I started hearing voices of another nature, dark and frightening. It was as if after such an amazing high, I was immediately to come down and witness the opposite to the same effect. Like when you have a night out and get high through drink or drugs, and awake the next morning feeling depressed and unbalanced; due to a hangover, comedown or both.

There were lizards trapped in between the metal mesh that covered the outside of the windows of my house to prevent them getting in, as there were ripped holes in most of these protective screens. In the kitchen alone, where there were three windows, each window had about three lizards in each.

Looking back I should have helped let them out, there were bone remains of some that had died trapped. To be honest I had and still do have a fear of them, but that is no excuse for leaving them to die. Most were quite small, about four inches long. One of those in the kitchen however was about three times as big and pure green, whereas the others were of a brownish colour. It felt like the demonic voices in my head were coming from the lizards. It is unfair to still assume that, just because the heavenly experience through the voice of my Uncle happened when the birds were there.

I can only assume now that my subconscious was entirely responsible for all of this, it was unfolding a message to my waking state consciousness to flee home before I changed my mind. I believe that the birds were somehow summoned by my subconscious or possibly by someone who has died and looking out for me like my Nana or Great Uncle Bob, or Great Uncle Mike and that the voice of my Uncle was from my memory of his voice and was set off in my conscious mind coincidentally by my subconscious to utilise the scenario to get a message to my conscious self. Or the birds arriving that day as they did were just a fortunate coincidence, for nothing like it had happened on the many other times I had sat outside alone. The lizards I believe now, had no part in it, other than they were there and became the focus of my fear.

The voices were not continual. At first, after the birds left, they became intense and I remember my vision blurred for a short while and I came close to hallucinating, or what felt like passing out.

When the fear and voices subsided a little, I was left an emotional wreck. I felt dirty and showered twice, trying to break myself out of the ordeal. I didn't know what to do, who to call. I was due back to work ages ago and feared the worst if I contacted them now. I really didn't want to be hospitalised here. In truth, I didn't want to be hospitalised at all, I was afraid of secret conspiracies and believed that my current experiences were a sort of spiritual awakening. My fear was that I may be locked up forever. You see to understand how I felt, it is important to realise that at that time I really did believe the whole experience was real and was happening as it appeared to.

During one of the breaks from the voices I called a girl I hung out with sometimes. She worked in a designer clothes-shop at the end of my road. There weren't many shops, only that one and a newsagent next to it. I'm not sure exactly what I said, I certainly didn't tell her I was hearing voices as she may have been scared. I hoped they wouldn't return while she was with me. In fact, I hoped that her presence would stop them returning. It did, she stayed and booked me a flight home for later on that afternoon. Then she helped me start to pack before going back to work.

I knew the Rasta that owned the shop, he was a nice guy, a true Rastafarian, married to a white British girl and they had a girl of around four or five years old. When I was on my own again the voices started coming back in waves, they were fainter than before and I could carry on packing in between them. During one of the voice waves, whilst in the bedroom trying to pack, my attention was drawn to the lizards again, trapped in between the slatted windows and the mesh. I opened the window, reached inside and cupped my hand around one, then quickly walked out of the room, along the hall to the living room and out onto the veranda.

The gate was wide open, left unlocked after Charlene had gone. I wasn't worried about security now, I had run out of weed anyway, after rolling the last joint that was still in my breast pocket, and I had now tidied the tray up. There was no evidence to be found that I smoked weed in the house or took illegal drugs of any kind, remember I hoped to return once I had sorted out my addictions. I walked down the path to the drive and onto the street, then I dropped the lizard and in a flash stomped my foot on top of it, onto the hot asphalt.

I hoped that by some form of sacrifice, it would stop the voices. It was dead, the voices had stopped. Probably just from the shock of picking up the Lizard, although I remember it not being such a bad feeling once I got through the fear of touching it in the first place. I went back into the house and resumed packing, I felt bad for killing the defenceless little creature. I wished later that I'd tried to let the rest out from their fatal entrapment, instead of being left to die.

Maybe the voices were coming from them and maybe I was able to hear their cries for help, through their own fears, of death. Through fear and the continued drug use, lack of sleep and food, together with the previous night's experiment with straining my vision, had put me into a highly sensitive animal like state of alertness. This was quite possibly the reason for my connection with the birds and lizards.

I had to get out of the house. I had far too much stuff to pack as I had bought clothes when back in the UK, it was difficult to decide what to leave. I had the feeling that although I wished to return, I would not. My friend Dan had left a book about Hitler. He had asked me to return it to the university where he had borrowed it from their library. He studied psychology and I think had just been interested in the man, maybe to attempt to find out what makes a man make such choices as he did.

Dan also asked me not to tell anyone he had the book, in case they didn't understand, and now I wonder what my friends, who packed up the rest of my stuff after I was gone, would have thought about me having it. I never did ask them.

12 DEPARTURE

Finally, I got the car packed and as soon as I was out of the house I felt better. The lady next door walked over and asked if I was taking another holiday. I quickly explained that I had to go home to sort some problems out and didn't think I would return, I still felt very anxious. I said goodbye and got in the car. I only had to drive to the end of the road just now, as I wanted to thank Charlene and my friends at the shop, for letting her off work to help me. They were really kind, they were street-wise too and I knew they could tell what I was going through, at least to some extent, having probably witnessed it before.

They knew enough people, as did I, who had similar anxiety attacks brought on by crack cocaine. Now, although I never took crack, I took enough coke to make it the same thing long-term, as the main ingredient is as the name suggests - essentially the same.

For anyone who has smoked weed and experienced paranoia, the anxiety brought on by too much cocaine is similar, but of a magnified intensity. What I was experiencing was even more intense, but in waves, as at that time I was not actually under the influence of either drug; just mentally and physically unwell, in terms of my body's nervous system being shot to bits.

One of the guys working in the shop asked if I'd give him a lift home. My flight wasn't for a couple of hours yet and they were due to close shop soon so I decided to buy a beer hoping it would calm my nerves. I went into the newsagent next door, bought two beers, one for my man, to whom I was giving a lift, and I supped the other one, whilst sat outside the shop. The beer quickly took effect, as I had eaten nothing all day. I began to relax to the soothing reggae music being played in the shop and the owner's daughter talking to me.

Although very young, she seemed to have the best advice. I can't remember exactly what she said, but she reassured me that I was making the right choice by going home. I told her nothing of my ordeal; she must have sensed my unrest, or maybe her Dad had explained something to her. It felt like a positive sign and had a calming effect on me.

We left the shop after I finished my beer. The guy's house was on the way to my work-place, which was my next stop, to drop the car off and get a lift to the airport. I had called my boss before I left my house so he expected me. They were due to leave work now too, being the end of the day. The lucky delay at the shop had meant that I would not have to face so many people as most would have left by the time I got there, this was an unplanned relief.

I hoped that the relaxed state would last. I had wondered how I would drive, but focussing on stuff like driving and having a conversation with company helped. Let's hope it lasts the flight home, I thought.

As we left Sunsetcrest, driving up the hill from the shop, a funeral procession approached and the whole road was blocked. I turned to my buddy next to me and said, 'That's it, the 3rd funeral in a week. This is the final sign and now I know what it symbolised… me leaving Barbados, the end of an era.' I asked him to tell my Rasta buddy, next time he was down at the shop, and explained that he'd know what I meant.

I never had the clarity of mind nor the energy to explain properly about the previous two funerals and strong feelings of déjà vu. I dropped the guy off at his house, gave him the rolled joint and a mobile phone that someone had left in my house and I had been carrying around in the car for a while.

Then I arrived at the works in Cane Garden, all the labour had left for the day and most of the guys from the office. A few supervisors were around still so I said my goodbyes after a quick hand over to the boss. One of my estimating buddies was working late and said he would give me a lift to the airport, as he lived down that way. He never usually stayed late so I was grateful for the coincidence and for his kindness. I think he probably waited for me on purpose, which was really good of him. I could have called a taxi, but the airport was a good distance away and would have cost me a fair few bucks. My boss was a great fella too and would have given me a lift. I regret putting him in the position I did and owe him an apology one day, seeing as he gave me the job.

Thankfully my thoughts had levelled out, my mind not racing, but feeling clear. My estimating pal came into the airport with me whilst I checked in, and he waited until I went through the gate of no return. Once on the plane, I vowed not to touch a drink and tried to relax. A lady sat beside me. I vaguely remember talking to her, keeping the talk light, determined to remain in a normal state of consciousness. The flight was through the night, leaving Barbados at around 5.30pm and arriving some eight hours later in London Gatwick at 6.30am London time. The time difference was five hours behind in Barbados.

During the flight I dosed, but never slept properly. I remember watching the approaching sun rise above the horizon. Just before the dawn when the sky was still pitch black, I must have looked out of the window after dozing and been in a semi-sleep, or I was hallucinating, because I saw the stars fall out of the sky and into the ocean below. The skies were cloudless for the entire journey that I was staring out of the window, I had been looking intently at all the stars, and when they fell from the sky, not one was left up there, just blackness. It happened very quickly. I saw lots of streams of light pass by vertically, as each star fell at the same time and disappeared below us into the sea.

13 ARRIVAL

Following a thorough search of my bags, given that I had so many probably, and travelling alone, I walk out of security at Gatwick airport and buy some lilies to take home for my Mum. I haven't planned this part of my trip, nor any of it actually, but the flight was the easy part. I now had to find my way from Gatwick airport to Devon where my folks live.

Having not really slept properly since the night before I saw the Demon, I am faltering and unable to think properly, plus my mind has taken a beating with the on-coming psychosis which I am worried about, but with having no previous experience to relate it to, I am unsure what is going on, or what to expect.

I haven't eaten anything since the evening before the day I left, with all of the adrenaline, I just wasn't hungry. This lack of care for myself, through my lack of awareness for my basic needs, contributed to another series of panic attacks, voices in my head, dizziness and lack of ability to co-ordinate myself and find the right route home. Relying on old memories I picked the route home to Devon. I must have gotten to London-Paddington and took a train to Reading. This used to be a route I'd take to Devon years ago, if my ex-girlfriend from Swindon was coming too. She would meet me at Reading.

However, this route went to Exeter which is considerably further to my parents than Axminister, the closer station that I would usually have gone direct to, from London-Waterloo.

Still not eating, and drinking coffee with sugar, I suffer a coffee hangover with low blood-sugar and burst through my consciousness into a waking nightmare in Reading train station. I've just stepped off the train from London, entered a cafe and am now sitting on a bench on the platform. I feel like I should know what to do and what platform to go to, I try reading the monitor above me, but it's no use. I have this intense fear that there are ghosts watching me and the oldness of the train station is really freaking me out. The voices in my head are like several radio stations interfering with each other and I can't make out anything useful from the babble of different voices.

Refraining from speaking aloud and scaring any passers-by, I ask the voices quietly in my head for answers, but there are none apart from the occasional "fuck you" in reply. Some of the voices take over intensity and loudness and feel like they are addressing me directly, but only for a moment and then it's back to continual chatter. With all this noise in my head I haven't a chance of finding my way. I notice a pub in the distance, beyond an intermediate platform, a pub I recognise and then remember is on platform four, which is the one I used to catch the train to Swindon from. I decide to hike all my bags over to there and on the way I realise that it might be a good idea to try the ticket office and find out what platform I need. There is a massive queue and I give up, walking to platform four where the bar is.

The bar was closed and so I sat on another bench, resting from carrying all of my gear over the bridges and up and down steps. Not a good way to travel with so much stuff at the best of times. Then I hear an announcement that the train on the adjacent platform is about to depart to Guildford. I think I asked someone if it went to Axminster, which it definitely wouldn't have done, but because of my mixed-up head I was confused. What I really needed was the

Exeter train. Well, in my head I heard this person say they thought it did go to Axminster, whether they really did say that though, I'll never know. Boarding the train with all of my luggage and bunch of lilies in hand I feel a little closer to safety.

Although subconsciously I knew I was on the wrong train and was definitely nervous about something, it didn't dawn on me that I was until the end of the line, Guildford.

Although the voices stopped on the train, I was feeling intensely anxious and so absorbed with fear that it made me feel angry with the pain of it. I remember pressing my finger and thumb nails into the stems of the lilies in desperation. Now I'm unsure if this had any reason for them wilting or if the train was too hot, but when I got ready to get off the train I realised that the flowers looked like they were dying.

I took this as a sign, together with the fact that I had caught the wrong train, that possibly I was making a mistake going home. You see, my parents at this stage were blissfully unaware of my predicament and I did fear that my Dad and I might fall out over it all. In my mind this would be a good excuse for him to divert his problems from himself. Reality is, he would have helped me no-end and forgiven me for my self-abuse and illegal behaviour, because I am his son and he loves me.

The train station at Guildford is small, so I leave my bags piled up to the side of the ticket office, there is no one in there but, they can't be long, I think, and the telephone box is just outside. I phone my Mum and tell her the good news. I tell her not to worry, that I have come back home, but also that I have had a spiritual experience and need her to call Uncle Frank for me. Remember, Frank's voice in my head that I thought came from the bird, told me not to tell anyone of the experience, so in a coded message to Frank I ask something, I can't remember what, and ask her to call me back with Frank's reply.

Obviously he didn't have a clue what was going on and was unable to answer whatever riddle of rubbish I had asked my Mum to ask him. This answer though, in my mind, said that I was making a mistake going home. I explained the same to my Mum and asked her not to worry. I think I explained that I needed to get off the drink alone, not worrying her about drugs at this stage. It made sense because Dad was still drinking and it wouldn't have worked anyway. I said I'd be in touch and was sorry to worry her and that was it, I ran out of money in the call box.

Back in the train station to get my bags and catch the next train to London and then Scotland, I have had a master plan. Only one of my bags is missing, a small Helly Hansen satchel I've had and loved for years. It had many valuables in, such as my full CD collection, a 50mm Nikon camera lens and lots of things of personal value at that time.

Annoyed with myself for being so stupid I make a note to be more careful. The train comes and I have a pretty uneventful trip to London. Arriving back in London I find the day is quite warm, the sun is out. I feel more relaxed and I feel glad to be back in the UK. I notice a site outside one of the stations I'm in and am sure that my old friend Dave from Taylor Woodrow is working there. For a completely crazy reason, basically no reasoning, I wander out of the station with all of my belongings and go into one of the construction sites, looking for Dave. I have no joy finding him of course and make my way back into the station.

My master plan either eluded me, or the call for a drink more likely, enticed me into a station-bar, but that's exactly where I end up until nearly closing time. Several Guinness later and I am back on my way, but to where, I can't remember. In the pub I recalled my master plan to go to Scotland. I realised I had to buy camping gear and warm clothes if I was to survive the cold winter. I planned to buy all this in Glasgow, on route to the western isles.

However, I ended up wandering the streets of London. The busyness of the city together with my sleep deprived, starving self, and alcohol hangover, plus cold turkey from no drugs scenario was really kick-starting the psychosis again.

I think leaving the pub, possibly in Victoria train station, I had a vague idea I needed to head to Kings Cross to catch a train to Scotland. On leaving the main station to catch the tube, my ticket was swallowed in the machine and I couldn't get back in.

What I know for certain is that the feeling of fear, mainly from a feeling of being watched by some dark force, was confusing my thoughts and preventing me from thinking straight, as was the alcohol, no doubt. I had experienced some oneness in the pub with a guy playing the gambling machine. Watching the flashing lights of the puggy machine didn't do me any good and I felt like we had been talking telepathically, at least I don't remember saying anything to him that would make him act odd toward me, but he kept saying stuff that made me feel like he was some kind of secret agent, a mind reader, or knower of another world. Similar to Harry Potter, my mind was thinking along the lines of magic, a dark underworld in London. The first Harry Potter book came out in 1997.

That year I returned home from Barbados, I believe the fifth book had been published: *Harry Potter and the Order of the Phoenix*. At this stage I had not read any but, my sisters were interested and at that time I didn't realise adults would enjoy them so much also.

On the streets feeling very exposed, I pull my cap down low covering my eyes from passers-by and attempt to heft my bags across town until I come across another tube station I can get into. Somehow I lost my cap; I think someone swiped it, probably took advantage of my mental-looking state.

I found a tube station before they closed, or managed to get back into the one I had exited, and boarded a tube towards Kings Cross. All I remember though, is having to get off early, I think at Euston, because the cha-ching cha-ching of the train moving along the rails commenced a left, right or opposite phenomena that proved to drive me to the depths of insanity. This happened again and again in various forms over the following fortnight. The current reality at that time however, was a feeling of ascension to a God-like place, a feeling of ultimate knowingness, an awareness of the fundamental basis of life, an unexplainable feeling of ultimate knowledge. The feeling was so intense, it was frightening. Voices matched the feeling in growing intensity, some scarily demonic, and questioning who I was, if I was the messiah, if I was Jehovah.

As the feeling and voices intensified my hands began to sway from left to right, tic-toc, tic-toc, tic-toc. I began to speak in a similar fashion. I wanted to get off. I couldn't stop the intensity growing, it felt like I was going to explode out of my body and lose myself, possibly die, possibly just go completely mad. I feared this more than anything. This was a nightmare occurring on a packed tube, one late evening in the middle of London. Although I wasn't dreaming, I was awake and scared to death.

Once out on the streets again I wave down a taxi. Only I don't really know where I am going now. Kings Cross and Scotland is at the back of my mind, out of reach. I had hoped to go to a remote island in Scotland, a place I have been to with my Uncle Frank previously. I had believed he was the bird for sure and that he might meet me on the island and help me cope with whatever I was going through.

The taxi driver got annoyed with my lack of direction and failure to give an address. I was so close to Kings Cross and being able to board a train to Scotland. The ironic thing was, I think I had been in that very station in the morning on the way to Reading.

It was getting late and my mind was in pieces. Old memories were all I had now, my short term memory was completely shot. So I gave an old address in west London and after an expensive taxi jolly jumped out in Hayes, Middlesex, outside an old local pub I used to go to with my old Irish girl housemates. There are two guys talking at the door, the pub has long since closed for the night. The guys look like they are on drugs, they are eyeing my bags and acting really weird. I don't talk for long, as one guy kept his ear phones in and was dancing on the spot anyway. It starts raining. The nightmare is never ending. I walk around the pub to the BP garage, buy some crap through the security window and ponder my options.

I manage to catch a bus here, in an attempt to reach Northolt tube station which isn't far, for I have had an idea that my friend Stu will most likely be staying with his girlfriend Louise who lives opposite the tube station.

The bus doesn't go all of the way though and I end up in a place I don't recognise. A kebab shop is tidying up for the night and having sat out in the rain waiting for another bus I am drenched and shivering. I changed my clothes in their shop; they were really sound for letting me do so. The rain had stopped and I find a bus stop that has a route to Northolt, yes, finally a break.

Eventually a bus comes and I board, asking the driver to make sure I don't miss my stop, explaining that I am totally lost and anxious. He keeps his word and finally I feel like things are going right, I step off the bus at around 4am. I walk across the road to Louise's Mum's house. She knows me from her visit to Barbados and I hoped she wouldn't mind me dropping in at this hour.

She does mind. Stu comes to the door, but first, she opens the window above the front door in her bedroom and recognising me starts shouting at me. I apologise profusely, explaining my situation and she calms down. Stu makes me a cup of tea and listens to my messed up story. I beg him for a lift to Devon explaining that I can't co-ordinate myself anywhere and eventually he agrees after failing to talk me into having a sleep first, which would have been the best thing to do. At least I would have remembered my decision to go to Scotland. Still, things usually happen for a reason.

So we head off to Devon at around 5am and all is well until we are on the motorway and I start having the feeling that I am experiencing telepathy with Stu. It feels like I am him, that I know all of his past. Then I hallucinate and find myself inside the car driving in front of us. My whole sense of bodily awareness left me for a short time and I felt like I was just consciousness floating around.

All of a sudden I am back in the front seat and Stu says he thinks we'll have to drop by the hospital in Basingstoke because he is worried about me and explains that his brother James had been through something similar. For the second time that day I beg him, I plead with him not to take me to a psychiatric hospital. It feels like Stu has been possessed, not me, he won't listen to me reasoning with him, his mind is made up.

PART 2 - PSYCHIATRIC MONOPOLY

14 BREAKOUT OF BASINGSTOKE I

'Oh man, I can't take it sitting here listening to these voices, I wish Stu would come back. Why can I hear what everyone is thinking, too much, too much, none of it makes any sense and my head feels like it's going to explode!'

I'm standing in a small square room, Stu is just outside and around the corner at the reception desk of Basingstoke's hospital. I'm waiting whilst they decide what to do. Then I break for it, the door is ajar and I know the way out. I run around to the left with the desk to my right. I can hear Stu shouting after me, I know he means well, he's been up since I woke him at 4am and just driven fifty miles.

Part of me wants to stop, to explain, but I know this is my only chance, so I leg it. I run down the hill out of the grounds and soon find myself on the side of a dual carriageway. I continue walking and now find myself quite far along the grass verge. Traffic is zooming toward me to the left and my thoughts are racing. The voices have gone for now at least, must have been the people in the hospital, I think. I have the thought that I could continue walking, all the way to the coast and seek a boat to take me away from the UK, to where, I don't know. I have no money, no cards, they're all in my bag which I've left in Stu's car. I am lost. I feel helpless, but there's no way I'm going back to that hospital. If I don't understand what's going on, they won't. I know they'll lock me up and throw away the key.

15 DUAL OF THE CARRIAGEWAY

The thought of walking into the road hit me like a train, it nearly made me turn there and then and throw myself into the carriageway of on-coming traffic.

Knowing it's not like me to even consider something like that, the worst part being, that I was so lost in my own anxiety I couldn't even think about who is in the cars, who's lives my irresponsible actions would cost.

Sitting down on the grass cross-legged, my back to the cars, I try to block out the roar of noise coming from the continual passing of cars at eighty odd miles an hour.

Luckily overcoming the odd, out of character urge, I sit there with my back to the traffic, praying for strength and trying to meditate; though at this stage, I don't know how yet.

I think it involves pushing my thoughts away and making my mind blank so I use all the mental power I have left, which isn't much, and I force the urges out of my mind.

Finally, the realisation comes into consciousness that if I end it this way and kill someone else in the process, that all hope of redemption is lost. Feeling deep down that I can't knowingly hurt another being, I manage to get up and walk back the way I came, thinking

'I've got to get away from this dam road'.

Passing the slope where I came down to the carriageway from the hospital, I pick the pace up, but not a run, it looks bad enough walking along the side of a dual carriageway without drawing any more attention to myself. After the yoga meditating posture I'm sure some phone calls have been made already and I fully expect a police car to appear at any second.

To my right, across the dual carriageway road a tall shiny building comes into view, with modern reflective glazing. An office block likely, but my mind is racing and the fear has taken over, I'm losing control again. No voices as such, none that I can remember anyway, but I felt a strong pull toward this building.

'What could be doing that, is it because it's across the road, am I trying to kill myself again?' I ask myself.

Feeling that people were looking at me from behind the reflective windows, they probably were, and thinking what's this head case doing? I'm so far gone that I start to believe aliens are in the building, I really did feel that I had to walk up to the front door, to check.

God knows why!

Totally lost it!

Managing to keep to my side of the road, walking along the verge until a slip road appeared and led me off the main road. Being too disorientated and in fear of the road to attempt crossing it I continued along until the end of the slip road.

16 MEETING THE WIZARD

Now from this point on the side of the entrance to the slip road until I find myself in Basingstoke bus station I can't remember a thing, I gather I just kept walking along the easiest route.

Next thing I know, I'm waiting for a bus but I have no money and no place to go. The hours pass by and the buses come and go. I think I looked like anyone else waiting and strangely, was not tired or hungry, but with no money I had no idea what to do.

I'm sat on a bench and a lady who looks almost identical to my ex girlfriend's mum, who happened to live not that far away, in Swindon, and worked in Reading, sat next to me. I thought it could be her, but it wasn't, she would have recognised me anyway. There was a buzz around this lady, not just the feeling of having bumped into someone I recognised because I knew it wasn't Jan; it was maybe what she was about to tell me or at least what I heard.

She turned and spoke to me. She told me that a young man would return to this shop today seeking the answer to a prophecy and that he would find his answer. As I looked to my right to listen to her, I saw the small newsagent just beyond her. If the lady and I spoke more I do not remember and I do not remember asking anything specific, I was in awe of her unexpected message

I walk into the wee newsagent shop under the premise of looking around, I have no money, as you know, and it must look odd just staring at the shelves. What am I looking for? What am I expecting is going to happen, am I waiting for someone to speak to me? The lady outside the shop must have meant I was the young man, why else would she tell me something so random?

I recognised bottles of Iron Bru on a shelf on the back wall, not seen these in ages I thought; then looked down and saw sandwiches on the shelf below. Had I had money I could have bought something, to look normal, but was still not feeling hungry anyway. Then I walked out of the shop and caught the eye of the shop assistant, just one lady behind the till to the right of the door. There were packs of cigarettes behind her, Regal Kingsize I recognised. Another thing I'd like to ask for, but no money and I didn't really want a smoke either, just to find out what was going on.

I think I may have walked in and out of this shop, repeating the same procedure two or three times, or more. Each time getting more paranoid that the lady in the shop would be wondering what I was doing. If I could have explained without sounding crazy I would have. Unfortunately, she was scared anyway. I remember the look on her face; she was probably thinking I was scoping the place out for a robbery and that I was crazy in the head.

She got the last bit right then! For the next event I can surmise now that someone, probably the shop assistant, called security.

I've entered the shop again, I'm looking at the back wall, I turn, and from the corner of my eye catch a large figure dressed all in white standing in the doorway, I turn back to face the Iron Bru and try to think.

Now if my memory serves me correctly, I had, in my earlier visit to the shop, had a feeling, maybe a voice in my head, that I was going to have to punch someone before the day's out. Strange, I know. Possibly my subconscious working again, of course, it knew what was going to happen as any normal, conscious person would, that security are going to be on their way.

Now for me to get help and be hospitalised, this was a solution, albeit an unfair one for the security guy. At the time my consciousness was not aware of this, I was like an actor in a play with no knowledge of the script, literally scratching my head hoping a sensible thought will come!

Slowly, and trying to look calm and casual I turn the other way, catching the look of the shop assistant again and not looking directly at the guy in the doorway. There is no one else in the shop now, the shop assistant looks like she doesn't want to be there either; another minute and probably she would have been ushered out too.

As I walk past her the intensity of fear has nearly overcome me and I hallucinate, her face looks almost lizard like, I can't make out her features at all. Just a lizard staring at me blankly. Weird. I look ahead now and face the door. Another man has come to the doorway and beyond the two I see one more outside, all dressed in white. Maybe they just had white shirts on, but if a lady's face just changed into a lizard's then they could have been wearing anything right.

I'm almost at the door, they aren't moving and the gap is almost taken up by these two big blokes. The one on the left takes a step inside toward me, but I'm stepping toward him. We're nearly in each other's space – then my own voice, inside my head, loudly informs me

'PUNCH NOW! PUNCH NOW!

So I respond by immediately raising my right hand and move faster at the same time, so I'm throwing myself out of the door whilst leading with a heavy right punch, all my focus and attention is on the guy to the left, who is closest, and my punch lands square in his face. I hear the smack, but he doesn't go down, just lolls back a little, enough for me to push myself out of the door-way and shoulder the other guy out of my way.

I am barely out of the door and the third man jumps on my back. I hit the pavement with the weight of him and am now shouting in fear as loud as I can.

"ARRGGHHH!!!!!!"

My mind is racing.

'Who are these white cloaks? Why are they trying to trap me in a shop?'

With all of my strength I try to get up, but the guy is still on my back and now has his arms tightly around my neck. I am still screaming, no words are coming out, just shouts, I want people to know what's happening, I fear I am going to be taken off by these strangers, unaware at this moment of who they are. My shouting drains quickly as the arms around my throat tighten and then, following one last effort to resist and get up, everything goes blank and I pass out.

Did I just die? It feels like it, I feel elated and free. I'm floating somewhere, I don't know where. I feel so happy I could cry, but I do not feel like I am in a dream or in a body anymore. I am in an expansive place with no limits, just openness, fearlessness; all pain forgotten, no longer relevant.

I cannot remember much of my surroundings, only a sense of either being in a dream or really leaving my body and of floating upwards. When I got to the end of my journey I was standing next to a dear friend and in front of us an old wise man stood. Old, I could only sense from the all knowingness about him. He was, in fact, ageless, indescribable, maybe not even a man. He introduced himself as The Wizard and he proceeded to give me a new name, whereby I took the second name of my good friend standing next to me. We were married here in a sense, not the kind of romantic wedding between couples on earth, more of a re-birthing ceremony with my friend as a witness.

At this stage I really did think I was passing on, I did not assume that my earthly friend had died nor believed her not to be there, it was so dreamlike, like she was just a formation of my subconscious, which, of course, I now realise, was all it was.

17 THE INFAMOUS BLUE BLANKET

I cannot remember now if I was aware in the dream that I had been choked, but when I awoke I remembered both this and every aspect of the dream and I really was crying, in happiness. It most probably was a dream. However, when I awoke I definitely believed I had just had an out-of-body experience and been re-born.

All fear had gone and so too had the three, white dressed, security guards. I however, was lying in exactly the same place, but on my back now, with a blue fleece-blanket laid over me. I would see blankets like this again.

Two kind police men stood next to me. I heard them before I saw them. I didn't know what to expect, but it wasn't more violence. The reason I couldn't see them was when I awoke I pulled the blanket up over my head. I wasn't embarrassed or aware of anyone watching. When I did get up there was no one there, but the policemen.

I think I was surprised to be back and part of me didn't want to be, even though lying there I felt safe and more relaxed than I had in days. I felt overwhelmed from being given another chance in life by the Wizard, who I associated with God - a new name, a new life.

When the police asked me if I could move I just lay there with the blanket over my head, in silence, in waiting. They kindly and gently lifted me up and escorted me into the rear of a small police van. There was only enough room for one in the little, caged area of this van, it was tiny. I remember us pulling away from the bus station, me in a little cell on my own looking out the rear window. It was maybe just a bus station, but not to me. It was a new beginning, my new birthplace perhaps.

We pulled into familiar surroundings, Basingstoke hospital, where I was earlier this morning. A team in waiting greeted me in a room immediately to my left as I entered through a single door, with just one of the policeman. I was not cuffed nor do I remember them asking me if I would come quietly, my demeanour must have been quite obvious. I was happy, but sad, a broken man in the eyes of any onlooker, and despite whatever I felt, that was what I was, broken and at deaths door. Whether or not I really had crossed that line yet, or just imagined it, it really didn't matter.

It wasn't the same entrance, but I definitely knew where I was. The sleep on the pavement had calmed me and my experience overwhelmed me still. So much, in fact, that I could not pretend anything other in front of these people, doctors I was sure, of how I felt. So real was my experience that when the leading talker, an oldish lady across the table, asked my name, I gave her my new one!

This time the hospital staff were ready. The lady psychiatrist asked me if I remembered being here earlier in the day. I said I did, knowing that, apart from whatever Stu had told them, they knew nothing about me or what I had experienced, other than whatever the police had just told them. Still, I had just given them a fake name and when they asked was I sure that was my name; I explained how it had just been given to me. Of course, by now, from Stu and whoever else they had spoken to, such as my parents, they knew exactly who I was. I confirmed my true original name anyway.

The room was full of people, all sitting down, but only three or four around the rectangular table that I was sitting at. The policeman sat to my right, a bit further than the psychiatrist was from me, to my left. I think now, from later experience, that there were other less senior, possibly trainee, psychiatrists in the room (two to three), a nurse or two and maybe a social worker, all sat quietly in the background, observing.

There were approximately seven people in the room, including the policeman, and then there was me. Everyone was looking at me, waiting for me to spill the beans. No questioning from anyone other than the oldest-looking lady psychiatrist. Let's call her Jean, but note I never learnt any of the doctor's first names, certainly not the senior ones anyway. It was always just 'Doctor', at least that's how I went with it.

The policeman, a youngish late-twenties man, informed me not to worry about the incident in the bus station, that the man I hit was a security guard and was not pressing charges considering that I wasn't well. I don't think he worded it like this exactly, but that was the jist of it. Although I was on a cold-turkey trip, I knew the facts, that I was not myself, and my mind was impaired.

So I accepted that I was now well-and-truly in the heart of where I dreaded to be, not treating it as rehab, but a place where I had my reservations. I had learnt through my dabbling with illegal substances that life was more complex than most people thought. I fully believed that not all of my experiences were just the drugs and if any place had real life experience of these kinds of outlandish abnormal events, it was one of these places.

'So what secrets am I at risk of unfolding?' I thought to myself.

At first, when I came in the door and everyone was sat down, waiting, it was so surreal, I couldn't help myself answer with a different name, it was like I was drugged, but I know it was just the overwhelming feeling of my experience.

After the policeman explained that the man was okay and not pressing charges, I regained a little control of reality and also of how I sounded to others. So I gathered my wits as best I could, and answered honestly, but not giving more info than was necessary.

First they wanted to know about my experience with the wizard and as I went in to more detail the policeman sucked up the story so much I couldn't help myself giving a full account of it. When I finished he actually told me that a man called David Blane, a self-confessed Wizard had, in fact, just escaped out of a clear box of glass, suspended above the Thames, that very weekend! I knew nothing of this and explained I had just flown back from a long stay in Barbados. This was where I reined-in some control. The birds, possibly my uncle, who I had not spoken to yet, to confirm otherwise, had told me not to speak of that experience. Still, I admitted to the cocaine taking and weed-smoking.

There was no physical searching or even asking if I had drugs on me. I explained how I had left Barbados in a hurry, after admitting alcoholism to my employers, and now sought to get off both alcohol and the drugs. After what seemed like a long silence and observational period I was informed by Jean that I was being sectioned under the mental health act, although just a preliminary observational section for now, to ascertain the nature of my condition.

18 THE DICE & THE CHAIR LEG

I was given a room next to the staff room. I think they conveniently keep this room free for first-timers for closer assessment, especially if they are not sure of your temperament. They expect problems during the settling in period, I would imagine.

The place was packed, both men and women, generally young-middle-aged folks. Also, everything was as you would expect an asylum in a film to be, wobbly chairs, parts missing out of games, horrible old-fashioned décor. The bedroom décor was a little better, proper new solid door with a window, and little curtain too, for checking on you at night. A single bed to the right as you went in, was tight against the wall to the staff room, with a single wardrobe at the foot of the bed closest to the door. Directly ahead, on walking into the room, was the sole window to the free world, with a small bedside cabinet in front of it, adjacent to the head of the bed. The window ledge was just below the height of the bedside cabinet, about two or three foot off the floor.

After two mental painful days and nights that have merged into one messy experience due to the anti psychotic drugs and calmers, I decided that I couldn't take it anymore. The medication did seem to be working. I don't know if it was that or just my frame of mind, but one moment I was almost completely normal and functioning fine, the next I was in a living nightmare. I had no warning of when the pain, the severe mental pain would hit me, I figured if I got out of this place it may not happen again, at least it hadn't hurt so much before I got here.

I sat on the floor of the communal living-room area. No-one else was there, probably too scared to be near me if they had witnessed me in the uncontrolled state, where my mind couldn't carry out the mere natural tasks of co-ordinating my body to get me from one room to another.

A game with some dice is open in front of me, I am not capable of understanding nor have the patience to play it, I am however, feeling quite clear of mind and maybe sharper than average on other things.

I am thinking about escape.

I roll the dice and it bounces off a chair leg. I sit there staring at the chair and notice that the chair is squint, the leg that the dice bounced off is loose.

This place is as fucked-up as the occupants, I think to myself.

Pocketing the dice, I get up and walk to my bedroom.

The hospital is quiet, where is everyone? Probably at dinner.

No one tells me when it is. I can't remember when I ate last. Fuck it, I'm not hungry. Let's find a way out of this-shite hole while no one's watching. I inspect the window in my room, it's the best possible option I have. The fire door in the corridor is most definitely locked and alarmed and there are people passing frequently; so never enough time to figure out how to escape.

On inspection of the window my heart picks up and excitement kicks in, the wooden frame is rotten and a crack has formed vertically to the left of the window. The idea hits me like a train again. I try to keep calm, but excitement is running through me. I walk quickly back to the communal room. Fortunately, there is still no one in there. The room is surrounded by glass windows so anyone walking past can look in. A quick look around to ensure no one is there and I bend down and take hold of the squint chair.

The leg is so loose that it comes out with ease and to my great satisfaction the dowel joint comes out with the leg, so that I now have in my hand a circular section, wooden chair leg with a much smaller circular dowel fixed firmly in the end of the leg that adjoins to the chair – perfect.

I slip the leg quickly up my shirt and tuck it into my belt and walk quickly, but casually back to my room, I am so excited.

This better work. It will work, I just know it.

I listen for noise. There is a major risk that any noise I make will alert the staff next door in the staff room, but it seems the ideal time. They are probably watching the dinner room. I can't hear any noise, but I really hope no one is quietly working next door. Maintaining my nerve, I take the leg out from under my shirt and insert the dowelled joint end into the crack in the window frame. It fits!

Gently now I apply pressure to the end of the leg and slowly enlarge the crack until I am able to insert the whole leg into it. I apply more pressure now, and after quite a loud crack the wooden window frame is ajar, glass still intact, and the gap between the frame and masonry window opening is good enough for me to squeeze my skinny frame through.

I close the curtains, hide the leg back under my shirt and head quickly back to the communal area. Great, no one is here yet. After a look around, to check no one is watching beyond the glass, I quickly install the leg back into the chair and walk back to my room.

Done it! Just need to plan my escape now.

19 BREAKOUT OF BASINGSTOKE II

My big bag, that I brought back from Barbados, that had also been in Stu's car earlier, was now in my wardrobe, unpacked. I have been wearing two pairs of trousers since I got back to the UK, because I've been feeling cold and just not right in the head! My credit and bank cards are still in my smaller backpack which is also in the wardrobe. Good lad Stu, he had left all of my belongings here. I can't believe they didn't take my cards though. I have two cotton jumpers that I took to Barbados and I'm wearing one of them. I pack the other one, a hoody, into the backpack. Unfortunately I don't have a coat. I do have some cans of juice, fruit and chocolate that Mum and dad left the day before when they came to visit. I pack all of it into my small backpack and leave the big bag in the wardrobe.

I decide to wait until after the drug-round and lights out. Noise should be minimum opening the window now that it is pried open, and there is usually a lot of noise at the start of lights out, with people not wanting to go to bed and the like. The staff next door are usually chatting away loudly too, so that should muffle any noise I make, and as long as I can fit through the crack in the window, I'll be gone in minutes. It's dark already outside and there's no way they'll know which way I've gone. I know I just have to stay away from the town and from people. I know too that Basingstoke is surrounded by beautiful countryside, as I remember changing trains here before, when going to Devon.

I do not recall having a meal at Basingstoke. I'm sure I did, but I can't remember the canteen area nor remember eating the night before I left. I remember the drug-round, taking my pills and climbing into my bed fully-dressed, with my two pairs of trousers on. I had my zipped, blue Tommy Hilfiger top on too, and had stashed my backpack under my bed-covers so as not to risk making any noise opening the wardrobe and going near the door with the curtained square window.

Lights out. I waited some minutes until the face at the window stared in to check I was in bed. He shone a torch beam in my face, as per the usual practice. I had my eyes half closed when he came to the window, and was trying to look like I was going to asleep already. Before the light shone on my face I closed my eyes lightly.

The time to go was now. I could hear noise outside the door, and from within the staff room next door. I hoped that the curtain to the staff room window was closed. I could see light coming from the window of the staff room earlier, when I pressed my face to my window and peered around the wall, before getting into bed.

I silently got out of bed and put my trainers on, making sure the laces were tight, and I was ready for running. I had got an extra pillow out of the wardrobe earlier and used it with my head pillow to beef up the space under the duvet to make it look like I was still in bed. I needed all the time I could get if I was going to get far enough away from Basingstoke. I hoped the hospital was on the edge of town, but I had no idea how long I would have to trek through the streets to find cover.

Within seconds from getting out of bed I was prying the window open with my hands. There was a small cracking noise, but nothing too alarming. I carried on and pulled the window frame apart just enough to squeeze my body through. I made sure that the external window curtain was closed behind me, so as to look normal when the staff shone the torch through the window to check on me later.

Hoping that I had judged it right, I squeezed my backpack out first, then head first, tilting my body sideward I squeezed out with just enough room to avoid getting trapped. Fortunately, the room was on the ground floor and once out of the window it was just a short distance from the concrete windowsill to the ground. A quick glance to the right informed me that the staff room curtain was drawn closed, result!

I did not turn back and look into my room, if anyone knew what was going on the curtain of the staff room would surely be open by now. I had to think on my feet and think fast. Though actually I was crouched down and spread out on all fours. I slipped my single-strap rucksack over my back and clipped the plastic buckles together at the front so it wouldn't come off, meanwhile glancing around the perimeter of the courtyard.

A quick mental risk assessment indicated that the only way out to avoid the staff room area, in case the curtain opened, was around to the left, but I wanted to distance myself from the building immediately. The view to my left showed me that I would remain within the hospital grounds if I took that route.

Watching and listening for security I silently crept forwards across the open courtyard. The area to the right was aligned with tall, dense fir trees and I immediately headed for these as fast as I could move, yet quietly on light feet. I was running now, heart pounding in my chest from the fear and intensity of the experience, the flight or fight response was kicking in and I was flying.

Fleeing the courtyard and the hospital grounds I reached the trees in no time. There was no fence, no wall or any other obstructions, just tightly knitted fir trees and low branches. I crawled quickly under the branches and moved carefully through the trees, protecting my eyes. This was my playground now.

London was scary to me, with the traffic, lights, noise and lots of people, but I grew up playing soldiers in the woods in Scotland.

I could creep up within a few feet of folk who would hide in the rows of drainage gullies on the forest floor. I could be just over the next mound that separated us, would act like a scout, then return without them knowing I had been there.

20 FOLLOW THE MOON TO NEWBURY

The tree boundary to the hospital was not thick, a couple to a few trees in depth. I crept to the edge of the boundary and happily gazed upon endless fields. What luck, this was meant to be, first the chair leg and the window and now the location and having picked the best exit.

The moon was shining and lighting up the fields. I ran as fast as I could and headed for the nearest bit of cover I could see, a small clump of trees far off in the distance, in the direction of the moon. I never looked back once, but ran with such intensity that I must have believed somebody could be on my tail. I was free and it felt amazing, I wasn't ever going back to Basingstoke.

Finally I reached the trees. I must have covered some distance already. I was only jogging now and sometimes walking because the moon was at the other side of the trees, over a smallish hill that I was now at the base of. The lack of light made it more difficult to cross the uneven fields safely and the last thing I needed was a sprained or broken ankle. I clambered safely over a wall and made my way carefully up the hill, entering the cover of sparsely spread trees, that had naturally sprouted over the years.

Almost at the top of the hill I crouched next to a fairly large-trunked-tree and peered over the grass mound. I could see a gently sloping, grass hill descending to more fields for as far as I could see in every direction; result. I looked back now for the first time and could only see the shadows of the trees near me, nothing beyond, just blackness. I let my back rest against the big tree and without meaning to I dosed off asleep. The drugs must have kicked in.

When I awoke, probably from feeling cold, the moon was a bit higher in the sky, but still in relatively the same part of the sky, so I figured I had not been sleeping too long. I took my hoody out of my backpack and put it on. I listened for any unusual noises and there were none. The night was clear and windless, the sky was really visible and the moon full, it had been the perfect night to leave.

Starting off down the grassy slope I left the trees behind and was soon on the flat, but slightly elevated, ground. Considering it was the middle of an autumn night, I could see for miles, thanks to the full moon directly ahead of me.

At some point I decided my best option was to use the moon to navigate me as far away from Basingstoke as possible. I had put in some miles already over these flat fields. I judged that the moon was a good omen, it had happened to be in the direction I was heading to, from the start of my escapade, when I made the burst from the wooded hospital boundary.

After a while of walking I saw lights ahead. I figured now that walking was fine, I was tired and weary from the meds. The lights were too big for a car, and after a while they turned and shone in the other direction. A fear gave rise, only a little doubt crept in, 'shall I change my heading?' I thought to myself. Visually I was not breaking any skyline, not walking along any hills on the horizon and even if I were, from that distance, without making artificial light I was invisible.

Whatever it is, I thought, will not see nor hear me, so I carried on. It soon became apparent that the lights were from a tractor. I was still too far off to hear it and as I walked on, following the moon, I realised that I was going to be quite a long way away from the field that it was working in. By the time I got down to near that level of terrain, still quite a bit higher, I could make out my bearings from the tractor to where I was heading. I also realised that a huge, thick, tall bush was completely separating my area of stubble field to the fields the tractor was working in.

Before losing the high ground I spotted more lights in the distance, following each other sporadically, not in a congestive manner. Definitely a road, I thought, probably a main road given the amount of cars on it at this hour. I set my goal now to reach that road before sunrise. So I had no more stops and slogged on. I say slogged, but really it was a pleasant walk. No worries for the meantime, no fears, just walking under the moonlight and starry sky and feeling free.

I must have zoned out whilst walking, because the next thing I remember I was on the road, walking in the right-hand direction from where I had been coming. I don't recall what made me take that direction, but I do remember that from the trek across the farmlands during the night, the cars had been heading in this direction. I think I made my decision then, it seemed to be heading still further ahead at the same time to the right, whereas the opposite direction seemed to be gradually heading backward to maybe where I'd come from.

The sun was coming up, promising a nice day. I was walking facing the traffic and on the other side of the road I noticed a bus stop, for buses headed in the direction I was heading. Apart from the bus stop and a Little Chef restaurant across the road, there were no other buildings as far as I could see; it was very remote looking with just one long main road through. I was feeling really hungry and needed cash for catching the bus, so I went into the Little Chef, after checking I had my cards in my bag still.

It was quiet, but a few people were in. Lorries were parked outside.

I ordered a full English breakfast and paid for it with my debit card and obtained cash back, for the bus. On the way in I picked up a Daily Mail newspaper and remember reading my favourite astrologer, Jonathan Cainer. I even kept up with his daily horoscope forecasts in Barbados through his website, and have done so ever since. Well recommended by the way, for inspiration, always a positive forecast with Oscar Cainer now taking over his late Uncle Jonathan's role and just as good!

So, sat at my table for one, looking out at the road, a steady flow of traffic building up, more so in the direction I was headed: Newbury; only a few miles down the road. It is seventeen miles from Basingstoke to Newbury. I must have covered ten plus miles during the night, across fields, fences, walls and forests. I've checked the bus time-table and Newbury is the last stop. Not many stops before it, so I gathered at the time I was close already.

I had stopped at Newbury train station many times to change trains on weekend visits to a small village in Wiltshire, called Pewsey. I also knew where Basingstoke was on the map and had a good idea where I had travelled.

What a result, I thought to myself. I remember all the uncanny coincidences solidifying my decision to flee to Scotland. There really were limited choices left now. I don't know where my passport was, maybe that had been taken off me.

My Dad, on his visit to the hospital, had, apparently, warned them that if there was a way out I'd find it, so maybe, for safe measure, Dad or the hospital staff took it. Strange that they didn't take my bank and credit cards, but they probably didn't think it a reality I would escape, or just presumed I had none.

So knowing the bus departure time, I finished my breakfast, took my paper with me and made out to the bus stop. I had freshened up whilst waiting for my breakfast and removed my second layer of trousers and put them in my bag, I didn't want to look crazy! They were darkish trousers, so Little Chef staff had probably not even noticed any signs of my escapades.

21 KINGS CROSS ST PANCREAS

Having been to Newbury train station many times I was familiar with the route to London Paddington, I knew the station platform very well. On my walk from the bus station to the train station I stopped at a pay phone to call my Rasta colleague in Barbados. I learnt afterwards that he told the boss, who then phoned my parents in Devon. They knew I was safe at least. I don't think I told my mate my exact whereabouts or where I was headed to. My family in Scotland were expecting me to call anyway, because the police had alerted most of my contacts upon learning of my escape.

At this point, in Newbury, my mind was surprisingly clear and focussed on what I had to do. I boarded the train to London Paddington, having bought a ticket to Glasgow Central, the place where I could get a train or coach to somewhere remote, away from people and police, away from chaos and stress. Glasgow I knew had lots of camping shops, a required visit, if I were to have any chance of surviving the winter.

The change via the circle line underground from Paddington to Kings Cross was smooth, and I boarded the train to Glasgow with no problem.

Fortunately, I stayed off the drink, maybe slept a little and the journey went okay. I was sat at a table, window seat, facing the front on the right-hand side and had a good view of the East Coast. I always enjoyed travelling by train and this route up the East coast has great views as the line follows the coast, especially in the North East of England, where the cliffs are high and the beaches magnificent.

A girl, Rose, boarded at some station in the North East and sat opposite me. We started talking and before long I had given her a short version of my recent experiences, leaving out hospitalisation and breaking out, so as not to frighten her or alert the authorities. I wanted her advice on something.

It was now getting dark and the distraction of the scenery had faded with the light. My thoughts had turned back to my predicament and fear was creeping back impatiently. I asked if she thought I should go cold-turkey on my own in a remote setting, away from temptation, or whether I should stop in on my family, my aunt and uncle in Callander. Her advice was to go to my family. It felt like the right thing to do and so I asked to borrow her mobile for a quick call to let them know to expect me.

At this stage the fear had shook my nerves again. I was no longer thinking clearly, it was more like following a subliminal instinct. The phone number came to mind without any hesitation, despite not having had to remember it for years.

My fear of whether I was doing the right thing, and of entrapment again, eased, everything was all too clear, but not in the way my conscious mind had hoped. I took that to mean that I was going to be safe, that my aunt and uncle would take me in and I could get better there.

Something that possibly secured this thought was probably a brief subconscious memory of sitting in my house in Barbados and thinking of options to change my life, when the thought of going to my aunt and uncle had first come to mind.

At this point I wasn't conscious of that memory, it wasn't until months afterwards, maybe a year after the event, that I realised this connection, whilst making a journal of my experiences. It was this journaling that helped me understand how my subconscious had worked to get me where I needed to be.

22 A STOP AT STIRLING

Having disembarked the fast east coast train at Edinburgh I bought a train ticket to Stirling. Trains run pretty frequently and so I was in Stirling probably within a couple of hours of making the call. The train pulled into Stirling and I got off and walked out of the station to find my aunt and uncle and their youngest son, my cousin, who was about twenty years old then, in their car just outside the station.

We drove for half-an-hour to Callander, where they live. On the way I told my cousin about the experience with the wizard. There was so much to tell and I wasn't sure what I should or should not say. My mind was racing, not knowing what to say exactly, but bubbling out rubbish anyway.

When we arrived at their home, I felt a nice warm feeling of being back in familiar surroundings and a sense of security. My aunt served me up a real meal and I sat at their kitchen table. They had lived at this house since I was around ten and it was like a second home growing up as my Mum would drive us over every few weeks. I noticed that they had laid a new laminate floor as I looked down from the table and took in the surroundings.

After finishing my tea there was a knock at the front door. I was still sat at the table when a policeman walked into the room. Another was just behind him, they were both young. I stayed calm, I wasn't about to cause a scene in front of my family. I considered the back door and legging it into the night, but it may include more violence and this policeman looked really nice. He let my auntie explain to me that she had been contacted by the police, informed that I may arrive and to notify the police as soon as they had heard from me.

The police had agreed to let my aunt and uncle bring me back from the train station and give me a meal before they arrived. I pretty much knew what was going to happen next and I surrendered to it, despite feeling anxious as hell.

My cousin asked if he could go in the police van with me to the hospital, but they said no. And so I reluctantly climbed aboard, no cuffs again just no options either.

23 RISK ASSESSMENT

At this point, I must explain the risks and give you the controls to avoid them becoming your reality. A detailed insight and exposure to the unknown world of madness will be revealed to you. Yes, I am talking to you the reader, whoever you are. If you are reading this book in the hope of changing your life in a positive way, keep reading and I will give you the tools to do so in the next section: *Rehabilitation*. The very act of explaining my experience can possibly be a lifeline to you in itself, by creating an environment for a similar experience, but I do not wish the pain I endured on anyone.

The knowledge of my experiences might be a trigger and cause your own story of madness, one that you may not be fortunate enough like me to come back from. There are people institutionalised in psychiatric hospitals, but there are also people who are not just institutionalised, they have no, or very little, control of their mind.

They may well be in control sometimes, but not for long enough to prove that they are sane. This should not make you fear going to hospital to get better as I believe if you can make the choice yourself to sort things out before it is too late then you can hopefully avoid what happened to me. If you can read this and understand it then you are capable of making the early steps to change, and yes, change is possible. It is a myth that people cannot change. Life itself is change. The book that helped me change is called *Change your Mind* and I will reveal all in the next section.

For now, please consider exactly what it is that you want in life, before continuing to read the next few chapters.

The risk of being exposed to my experience is that your subconscious mind will have enough information to piece together the pieces you need in order for your own painful journey to take place. It is therefore advisable to consider whether or not you really do want to change your addictive nature. If you do, or you have no mental problems of any kind then read on and please continue to the next section *Rehabilitation*, where I give you the tools you need to get better or help others.

This should keep you from experiencing something similar to me, and this is your control to avoid that risk. If you do have issues of any kind relating to drink or drugs (remember alcohol is a drug, just a legal one in our country), and you have no intention of changing your lifestyle, then my advice is to stop reading now and wait until you are ready. Otherwise you run the risk of going insane.

The immediate control responses I describe below will probably not help you even if you can remember them, which you won't because your thoughts will be jumbled. So to push my point once more, read the following at your peril if you have no desire to change. Risk assessment of this section deems the knowledge to be low-risk if you continue to read the next section and take up some of the controls I give you. These controls are not just in lowering the risk of madness, but in providing a positive change to your life, in ways that you can probably not imagine just now.

24 FALKIRK, WARD 19, PSYCHIATRIC UNIT

Once we arrived at the hospital it must have been pretty late, lights out anyway, because not a patient in sight. I was shown to my room pretty quickly. It felt very hospital-like. I didn't feel like I was in a prison, not yet anyway. It was just a secure ward, but one step away from the criminal mental hospital, in a place not far away, called Carstairs.

My auntie and cousin were not allowed to stay very long and I went to bed. Another strange bed in another secure ward, not much more than 24 hours after the last one. The bedroom and ward as a whole were more modern than the Basingstoke one, not much more, but the windows were new. There was certainly no way of escaping out of them anyway, I thought to myself.

After a night on the run and another day's travelling I was so tired I would have slept anywhere. Not long after getting into bed a torch light beams through the window in the door.

'Yes I'm in bed', where do they think I'll be? Another breath or two and I'm asleep, a smooth first night, the calm before the storm.

The morning is fuzzy, I am anxious about meeting my neighbours. I don't remember eating and I don't remember talking to anyone. Anxiety takes over my rationale and I am just following a series of reactions to my mood of negativity. I seek to escape, but the place is in lock-down and my thoughts are racing, I have no control over them and I can't even consider the simplest of things. Full-blown psychosis is lingering again, not at the edge of my consciousness, but now within it. Yet I cannot recognise this, and had I been aware of it anyhow, I doubt that any difference would have come of it.

There comes a point when the thoughts race so quickly into each other that awareness of reality becomes distorted and fear consumes your entire being. This is where you become to feel helpless and scared. Helpless to make a decision to will yourself back to normal; scared that you will lose yourself completely and forget who you are. A dangerous place to be.

A little clarity emerges and I try the fire escape bar on the fire door. I have been eyeing the two fire-exists all morning and no one seems to be paying me any attention. I'm sure they must know what I'm thinking and I know my half-cocked efforts at escaping are fruitless, but it's been such a painful day already. Obviously, the door doesn't open.

I sit facing the door, in a cross-legged position, and I pray for it to open. I must have sat for hours.

All of a sudden my auntie is here, I know she can't take me home, pointless to ask. I must look in a bad way. I try to smile and be myself for her, but I think I probably portray but a shadow of my real self. We sit on the couch in the visitors area, near the front door, with all its high security locks, and to the opposite side of the nurses station, which is in an enclosed, square room with glazing to the nearest walls. The two far away walls are external and behind that, freedom. You cannot hear what is being said behind the glass. There are usually four or five people in there during the day.

Kindly, my auntie gives me some rolling-tobacco and some rolling papers. I think she gave me some chocolate and magazines too. I need a fag. She hugs me before she leaves and promises to come see me the next day.

The smoking room was also opposite the enclosed nurse's station, in fact, you could see everywhere from the station, except along the corridors where the bedrooms are. The building was like a cross with the kitchen and dining area directly opposite the front door and furthest away. The nurse's and doctor's room within the glass walls was to the left of the front door if looking into the ward from standing at the threshold, and where I had been talking to my auntie was to the right, with couch, chairs and a bookcase. There were also some couches and chairs that were placed strategically facing the glass walled-office, with a TV to watch, in-front of the glass.

In the middle of the room were some tables, that were usually there for visitors and for playing games. However, earlier that day they were moved down to the dining area and a big table-tennis table was set up. I had watched the table tennis for a while, following the ball with my eyes from side to side, trying to maintain focus on it. It was a relief for a while to have something to focus on.

The small smoking room was also enclosed in glass from about half way up, with timber panelling below, very similar to the nurse's and doctor's room, but it looked a lot older. There was a window in the far wall opposite the doorway, and it had a reasonable view of a hill in the distance, scattered with trees, but not too densely, so that you could make out the railway line, due to an unnaturally level embankment running along the top, within a small clearing of trees to either side.

25 COLD TURKEY

To the right of the window in the smoking room is a solid wall, with the kitchen area to the other side of this wall. There is a 90's mini hi-fi stereo player on a small table in the middle of this wall, not too dissimilar to the one I had in Barbados. At least it's not levitating, yet!

Between the table and the wall with the window is a comfy looking armchair. I sit in that and look out the window, having opened the tobacco pouch already, I roll up a smoke. Opposite me a man sits on a couch. He introduces himself, and he looks a little funny, almost pulling a face when he talks, as if he is acting. I wonder instantly if he is. Days to follow, I often imagine him being an insider, if you know what I mean?

Pretending to be ill, to learn about the patients and feed the information back to someone, possibly the Doctors. Or maybe a higher order, like the Freemasons or the Illuminati, who I'm yet to learn about. At this stage I haven't considered the Masons, but I was paranoid about some un-named organisation. I had the feeling that I was being watched. It was probably just the paranoia and the fact that I was being quietly observed by every Nurse and Doctor, all of the time.

The old guy seemed nice though, even if he did speak in riddles. He asked me why I was in. I told him the truth, there was no point denying it, the system knows why I am here anyway. He told me he was there for a similar reason; drug related I took that to mean, but he didn't elaborate. He was about fifty-years-of-age, maybe in his late forties, but more likely early fifties. I asked myself again, 'why is he really in here?' It didn't feel appropriate to ask and no one else ever asked me again.

After an exchange of few words, he gets up and leaves. I turn my chair to face the window, with my back to the ward, and I light up my smoke. I dream of being outside and imagine walking up the embankment. Whilst speaking to my new buddy there was a grounded feeling. Now that he has gone I feel really alone and bored. I roll another cigarette before I finish the one in my hand and I sit in the chair, chain-smoking, staring outside the window.

Several trains pass before someone comes to the door and tells me to come and get my medication. I must have missed tea. I'm not hungry though, my thoughts have all rolled into one again and I crave for some cocaine or weed. Having gone back into the smoking room, I sniff dust from the window sill, trying to get a hit. I know it's no use, but if I can only trick my mind into believing it is real, it's useless. Cold-turkey is returning hard and there is no escape.

Knowing that there is nothing for it but to ride this out I witness the pain in my aching head and realise that the aching cravings have intensified, and my thoughts have started racing again. All of a sudden I feel disconnected from reality, as I felt on the tube in London and in hospital in Basingstoke.

Every word imaginable enters my head in what felt like an instant. Feeling so unbalanced, my whole being feels like it will explode, and as the fear intensifies it feels that if I don't find an opposite word to say aloud to counteract the thought of the word inside my head, that the universe will implode and I will be responsible for ending everything.

This is because I no longer feel like my awareness is in my head, but instead, I feel connected to everything, to a higher consciousness almost. The reality of how quickly this change occurs from being mindful of yourself, to losing yourself into what feels like an awareness of everything, is so intense, beyond any explanation in words.

26 EVERYTHING IS EVERYTHING

I run out of words, I feel as if I have just gone through the entire dictionary, at least the one my brain possesses. If the thought hot came to mind I said cold, if light I said dark, if forwards I said backwards, and so on and on. I was stuck to the spot. I stood within the small, enclosed smoking room, and no one else was inside. I was also not aware of anyone watching from outside the window.

As my attempts to use my limited vocabulary fail me, my body starts to take over the act of balancing my mind by first twisting my arms in opposite directions, like a techno dance. This takes the pain away for a little while, as the opposing words did, but soon the thoughts beat me down again and I cannot maintain the balance, everything becomes fuzzy and voices enter my head. Lots of voices together in my head, so many that I cannot distinguish between them, I have a very, very light grasp on the here and now as the tiny part of my mind left to think for itself asks if these are the voices of the dead.

There is no answer, no communication, just voices, and then some become louder than others, more directed at me. I cannot talk to these, but I know the voices are directed at me. One really scary, demonic voice keeps asking me over and over again if I am the One, the reincarnated Christ, come back to earth in another form. Over and over again I hear this voice asking me in every possible different way if I am Jesus Christ.

I cannot walk anywhere at this stage, but I try turning on the spot for one cycle, then back in the opposite direction for another cycle and this seems to help. I now add the arm-movements in opposing cycles and I am literally dancing on the spot. It feels slightly better, but not for long. The voices subside a little, but the racing thoughts return. I am so tired, yet so wired. I feel that I could give up, but what then? Will the universe end? It feels like this is my turn to become the One and maintain the balance of the cosmos.

A sudden awareness is forming, that all beings, human and animals, all earthly matter and space itself is a mere illusion, maintained only by one being, for ALL is ONE and ONE is ALL. Therefore, all the people in the world and all the animals, all the planets and all the stars, everything in fact, is the same in essence.

'Everything IS EVERYTHING', 'I an I'. It is such a familiar feeling, and my whole life, and especially recently, seems to have been building up to this point. With this knowledge I feel that I have stumbled upon I cannot deny the trueness of it, it overwhelms me and fills my entire being. 'I am the One'.

If I do not try to maintain equilibrium in my being, I am going to break the illusion and lose everyone I care for, everyone will lose each other and there will be nothing again, just me (which includes you!). The feeling of loneliness and fear return, and a greater fear of losing my identity. The more the unbalancing thoughts sway me, the less aware I am of myself, I know that if I give up I will go completely mad, possibly taking out everyone along the way. If there is a chance of that, I must hold on and prevent it.

If that happens and there is only me, it won't be a person, myself as I know myself to be, it will be a common, supreme consciousness, possibly aware of itself, but not able to manifest into being. At least this was along the lines of how I felt. Words cannot describe the heightened awareness. It was as if I was aware of unimaginable knowledge of life itself, of the reasons for life and death that are usually completely incomprehensible to our waking consciousness.

The intensity of the thoughts push me harder still, my head is so sore and I cannot do anything else to stop the experience. In a last attempt to fight off the madness and being lost in the void of nothingness, I try a handstand, giving it all of my attention.

By focussing on maintaining a balanced body-position on my hands, the mental pain subsides, whilst the intensity of my focus keeps me in position. Finally, a nurse comes over and asks me to come down. I lose my focus and come out of the handstand, but it helped enough for me to break out of the madness. I regain some normal mind and body control and I take myself to my room.

This process of going mad and coming back out to relative safety continued in a similar way for nearly a week. I do not remember eating, or talking to anyone or going to the toilet, the week is a blur of painful memories. I later read a definition of madness, and from my personal experiences it matched it well and goes along the lines of: Going around in mental circles, unable to break the recurring patterns and coming back to an original thought.

The mental pain experienced from not being in control of your own thoughts is indescribable, more painful than any imaginable physical pain. Your head feels like it is going to explode. No matter how much you will yourself to do something, you can't. You are a prisoner in your own body.

Madness is like walking around in circles, unable to stop, but in your mind.

Although the madness may very well make you actually walk around in circles, amongst other crazy things, with illogical reasoning. The medical term is psychosis, the treatment anti-psychotics. Unfortunately, the meds don't work straight away.

It took a week for my medication to work. When it finally did I started acting like a normal person. By this stage I was already well known for my hand

and head-stands and talking to myself whilst dancing around, as if listening to music. I knew nobody else other than smoking room buddy and a young man, though a few years older than I, maybe ten years who knows. He would come into the smoking-room throughout the day and talk to himself. He would argue with people, and shout, as if they were in the room. He was pretty frightening, thuggish-like, but a welcome change.

At least I was aware of him. I would listen to him ranting, occasionally remembering people from my own past, long-ago, who had the same names as the people he talked to. Sometimes I would try and talk to him, but he just carried on as if I wasn't there.

Only once can I remember him talking to me directly. He asked if I could get hold of any pills. He meant ecstasy. I replied by saying I don't think so. Cold-turkey had turned into full blown psychosis and drugs were the last thing on my mind. Trying to stay in the here and now was the only important thing to me.

27 RADIO ONENESS

I feared the unknown existence on the verge of my consciousness, trying to break in at the least expected moment, such as whilst having a conversation with my smoking room buddy. I would be asking him something and the answer would come to me through the radio at the precise moment that I asked it. This was the start of a phenomena that hasn't left my life yet, I just pay no attention to it now. If there is any real coincidence there isn't any reasoning behind it that I can fathom. Although sometimes I must admit it does reflect my thoughts.

For example, I may be feeling a certain emotion about the subject I am communicating or pondering, and the word from the TV, radio, or from a nearby crowd of voices may reflect that very thought very accurately, and instantaneously.

This voice was of the radio-presenter, not of anything within my head. However, sometimes the oneness of the experience would bring on voices inside my head, usually asking me if I was Jesus again, or something along those lines.

If I answered, there was no recognition, as usual, no conversation, just a continual chant of questions and other meaningless babble, as if I had just tuned into an etheric radio station where ghosts talk. The voices that were not directed towards me did not sound as if they were communicating with each other either, they were just different sounding voices, saying meaningless things, usually negative and frightening.

One night during my first week, as I lay in my bed, the noise of the wind outside was consuming me. It was a hefty gale. The wind battered at the window and the branches of the trees swayed frantically outside. I observed this due to the artificial light from the street lights, causing shadows to form on the curtains.

Gradually I lost control of myself again, and all of a sudden I was no longer lying on the bed, but a part of the wind outside. I tried really hard to fight it, to come back to myself. No voices or racing thoughts this time, but an unimaginable sense of fear of losing my identity, of not returning to myself, overwhelmed me.

Another night a similar experience occurred. It was after another day in hell, of fighting madness through head-stands and opposing thoughts and actions. I had got to sleep, but when I did I was, all of a sudden, floating above my sleeping body and yet without a body. It was probably just a dream, but the fear and everything that I associated with madness was present. I was watching myself sleep, unable to wake up, aware of the knowledge of everything, but unable to do anything. When I recollected the experience it didn't feel like any dream I had ever had before.

Many nights were similar. When the faces of the nurses came to the door and shone the torch inside my room to see if I was okay, I would be lying with my head under my arms, trying to block out the noise in my head, of uncontrolled thoughts entering it. I only sought peace through stillness of mind, but with no techniques or knowledge of meditation at this stage, I was susceptible to my broken mind's attempt of resetting itself. The clutches of the illicit drugs-hold was leaving my body, and my mind was trying to regain some clarity. For things to get better, this process had to be endured.

I had abused my mind and body through continuous alcohol and drug-intake for years. Day after day, alternating between drink, cannabis or cocaine or all three. Since I was fifteen years old, not a week had gone by without a joint, and from sixteen and a half not a week went by without a good drink. When one started to get the better of me, I switched, but never a week without the other. I was completely addicted to being high. The only good thing about the moment I now found myself in, was that I did not seek to get high.

I asked myself many times since this episode: why did I have to always take things so far, why couldn't I pick up on the fact that I was endangering my life and others around me, and why did I have to get to the state that I was in?

Having met one or two people who had been in psychiatric hospitals, I knew the dangers of what I did. I guess I just didn't believe it would happen to me. And they seemed okay afterwards, so I probably didn't truly fear the consequences of my actions.

Now that I know what happens, the fear of ever losing myself again is, fortunately enough for me, enough to abstain from taking drugs and abusing alcohol. For either one, I believe, is capable of sending you crazy if you have had some previous exposure to the nature of the void of oneness. This exposure can be direct or via coincidental experiences of events and interaction between people, as briefly mentioned above and to recap as follows.

Such as having a conversation with a friend - you are thinking of something, possibly a question to ask; when you hear a snippet from another conversation nearby and it is directly relevant to what you are thinking. This can also happen via the TV, the radio and anything that communicates a message.

28 PINK RABBITS N' ICE

Staring out of the window, longing to be outside and trying not to listen for any oneness messages through the radio, although admittedly a part of me got excited when it happened, I sat in my usual seat in the smoking-room, contemplating. Maybe there really is more to this psychiatric episode than my brain just going haywire from the excessive hammering it has taken. Or maybe I just don't want to be branded crazy.

Could it be vanity? Maybe I sought to be higher than my station, secretly hoping to be God-like and have certain power over my destiny. Who wouldn't want to have some power over their destiny? Instead of bobbing around in the ocean like a mooring that has broken anchor; being swept around by the changing tides.

Remember back in Barbados, that's actually where the name Green Tea Buoy came from, a name I gave myself for the old-fashioned social media, whilst reasoning on-line in Barbados, on MSN messenger and Rastafarian blogs. It means one of many buoys, the name used for the inflated, buoyant part of the mooring that boats tie up to when they moor off the coast.

All the buoys are going to break anchor eventually and may bob around aimlessly for a short while, before grouping together as one and realising their true nature. That they are omnipotent and essentially the same in nature. Who will be the Captain of the buoys? That is the question isn't it? If we are all one, can there be a captain, a leader? How can we all be one and yet all remain individual?

Mental reflection of this question is a short-cut to a psychosis, trust me. The only way to understand is through regular meditation, and even then the answer will be unexplainable to another mind, our minds are not wired to understand this concept. Transcendence of the mind will provide awareness unexplainable by thought. Further, transcendence cannot be thought or imagined, same as non-attachment can't be practised, both come effortlessly or they don't come at all.

Safety in transcending via meditation resides in the knowledge that the physiology changes during meditation (refer chapter 43, Transcendental Meditation). These physiological changes create a basis for transcendence and for longer periods of experiencing pure consciousness to become possible. In essence the nervous system is refined, strengthened and normalised.

The experience of altered awareness gained through drug and alcohol abuse, is very dangerous, as you can, hopefully, now appreciate. It is however, a reason, I believe, for why many people continue to seek highs through abuse and why people return again and again to mental hospitals. Once these levels of awareness are experienced, it becomes difficult to avoid when getting high, especially on cannabis, as this tends to damage short term memory and brain wave connectivity and hence the mind finds other ways to communicate with itself and the nervous system.

So I'm sitting in the smoking-room and staring out of the window. My thoughts are controlled now, somewhat dulled-down actually, from the heavy medication, but at this stage I am not depressed, that will come later.

Right now I am just glad to be alive and well. I am glad for not being made to jump around the place and stand on my head to relieve the mental and physical pain of psychosis.

A young, slim, dark-haired man comes into the room, it's the first time I have noticed him. He sits down next to me, to the other side of the stereo, and takes out his rolling tobacco. I am a lot more social now that I am back to my functional self, so I introduce myself. The man introduces himself as Paul, he tells me about his journey here, he too has been in London recently and we kicked off a good conversation.

Right from the start we were friends and it just so happened that he was in the next room to me. My room is the last on the right of the right-hand corridor, when looking from the entrance of the ward.

Although we were not meant to be in each others rooms, Paul and I sometimes knocked on each others doors and went in for a chat. It was good to talk and not be observed for a change. Paul was pretty relaxed, almost appearing to be absolutely fine in fact, but I soon learnt what his issues were. They were very close to mine, although I did doubt that he had not experienced the pain, or at least not to the extents that I had; or else I do not think he would have remained as keen as he did to be in that world.

Paul often spoke of oneness. And he knew exactly what I was talking about, when describing the connection between the radio, or the TV, or just from hearing random words from people's conversations that seemed part of a subliminal message, seemingly taking place at the same time as your own conversation or thought process.

You may wonder how two completely separate conversations can correspond or somehow be connected in your mind, but there is no avoiding this uncanny, coincidental and regular phenomena. I still witness it occasionally in my sane life, as mentioned earlier, even though I spend a lot less time focussing on it and almost never look out for it now.

The problem with Paul was that he was transfixed with experiencing oneness, he sought it out all of the time and was depressed if it wasn't happening. He welcomed the voices too. I think, because everyone is different, they will experience psychosis differently, but the essential factors remain unchanged, maybe just the level of pain is different.

For Paul, I don't think his fears had been recognised. He didn't seem to understand me when I tried explaining about how near I was to losing grasp of my identity when the pain and psychosis was at it's most intense. When I felt that I was interconnected with the universe, as if all things were in me, and I all things.

He certainly understood the aforementioned expression and could relate to it from his own experiences. What I mean to convey is the point in which you peak and are about to lose your sense of who you are and feel that you will become integrated into everything around you. Sight is affected, everything seems to vibrate and become blurry, people's eyes become like ponds that you can see your reflection in and you have a feeling of interconnectedness, like you are the same person.

These feelings and experiences were the signs for me of being on the verge of madness. In essence, they were the reason sending me mad, and the fear is so intense you won't ever want to experience it. I know I am repeating myself here, but it is important to realise, as I tried so often to communicate to my friend Paul. Eventually I gave up and after about a couple of years we lost contact.

The description of this state is so hard to explain, yet, if you could imagine being able to ask the question of what it is; the answer would be within the question. For to know the very make-up of the question, would mean you are knowledgeable of its nature and hence the question alone would reveal the answer. Another cause of my own episode was pondering this very question, and at the peak of my psychosis the question would feel like it was sitting on the edge of my consciousness, waiting for me to ask.

The fear I experienced was so intense, it grew from believing that if I lost control and allowed myself to move out to the edge of my mind, I would become aware of the question that floated around on the edge of my consciousness. It felt like if this happened I would not be able to refrain from asking it within my mind and this fear ultimately was that if I just allowed myself to ponder the notion of the question (the question of life itself, the answer to why everything is why it is), then the reality of what we have on earth would implode in on itself, the whole universe would cease to exist, the dreamer (I) would wake up and realise that we are all part of the same whole (as per the Rastafarian expression *I an I*) and that we are all just living a partial dream, an illusory life.

It is not, I believe now, such a black and white fact of either we live in a real reality or we live in an illusionary world. However, I do believe that there is a lot more to our lives than we usually appreciate. From spending a week in psychosis, the reality of the experiences I had during this period were too real for me to just accept that I dreamt them all up in my subconscious. That's exactly what happened for most of the thoughts and reactions. However, I believe that some of my core feelings that were the cause of many of these thoughts and reactions, were not necessarily false.

On reflection, I certainly believe now that it was my subconscious that decided to unravel the series of events and use the coincidental happenings, such as the birds on my Barbados veranda, to bring me home and begin my recovery. The proof to me was when during my recovery, after discharge from hospital, I remembered the following: I was sitting in my house in Barbados, about two weeks before my departure and prior to my subconscious completely braking through to my waking consciousness. I had the thought of detoxing at my auntie and uncle's house, under their house-rules and care.

It was at the time that I had been trying hard to get off the cocaine and had flushed it down the toilet on a couple of occasions following a night out. I sat in the living room and gave myself a head check, to consider the possible ways of seeing this abstinence through, and one idea was to go home, but not to my parents in Devon as they still took a drink. This is where the idea of going back to Scotland to stay with my auntie and uncle came about, because my uncle doesn't drink and my auntie very little. This idea didn't come to much at the time it arrived on my consciousness, but it must have stuck for my subconscious to bring me home.

The contemplation of my experiences of madness helped my rehabilitation and in understanding my addictive nature. What I read and experienced through meditation in the following months, brought me to the following conclusion on the experience of transcending the psychosis of the mind. That this state of consciousness is beyond the mind, beyond thought; as fear is feeling based, not rational thought and so is pure happiness.

Both happiness and fear are at extreme opposite ends of each other. In life everything is on a spectrum of opposites. However, if you transcend the field of life, of opposites, you rise above or fall beneath, the spectrum.

This is the place I am trying to explain and failing, thankfully, or else I'd be sending us both mental. It really is not good to ponder something mentally, something that is unexplainable in words, at least not for too long anyway. Maybe time for a cup of tea, have a break and come back, I am, haha.

Back to the pink rabbit, Paul, he nicknamed himself this during his creative establishment of a peace campaign called *Party for Peace and the return of the Pink Rabbits*. What I don't think he realised was that you cannot describe this state of consciousness, and he didn't believe it to be out-with the spectrum of life, beyond communication. He was probably right in terms of the edges of it, the bit that your mind fears, right before you lose yourself in it from complete absorption.

Personally I have not focused very long on oneness, because anything that cannot be easily explained only has more chance of sending you mad than proving to be anything useful. The experience I do have of it from myself or other people, who have told me about their experiences, is similar to other psychotic phenomena like hearing voices; completely meaningless and useless information.

I have since come across interesting information in relation to Indian philosophy that provides theories that may explain the reasoning behind it, but to delve into this world without first providing a good grounding is not advised. When you meditate and practise yoga you do not seek to find these unknowns, but your mind and body become stronger, your grounding in reality becomes stable through healthy living.

Your diet and lifestyle naturally aligns on a healthier path and you then become in a better environment with less fear and more understanding. Your priorities change in a good way and the interest of the unknown does not diminish, it probably grows, but in a safer, more steady way, that suits your mental state.

It is possible that psychosis affects people so greatly, because it is so real to them (knowledge (of reality) is structured in consciousness). I can confirm that it is real, it was as real to me as is going to work now or spending time with my children. It is different, but real. The question of what is real is certainly posed to most people successfully coming out of psychosis and regaining normal, logical, rational, thinking. The problem is, not everyone comes out of psychosis. I'm not saying that these people are psychotic all of the time, what I mean is that they are in and out of that state of mind regularly and therefore struggle to have a normal life.

What keeps some in this state and some not? Possibly for some it is their will and a matter of support, for others they may just be too far lost in the first instance. I would like to think that Paul was not too far lost, but he certainly didn't have the will to be free of it, more so, he had the will to stay in that state.

Until you really want to be somewhere, you won't go unless you have to, and if you do go, you won't stay for long. So the doctors make him come back to sanity for a while, through drugs and possibly incentives of some kind in terms of financial or domestic matters, where to live for example. If he doesn't really want a normal life, he'll never have one. The problem is, he will go around and around in circles and in and out of hospitals, not getting anywhere. This is true for so many people that, unfortunately, are not conscious of the problem, at least not at the waking, conscious level. And if they are, subconsciously, which they probably are, it is too deep and mixed up with other core thoughts and issues to be recognised for what it is.

So the will to escape the circle of madness does not grow within the conscious mind to a sustainable level to have a practical effect. This is similarly true for addiction, for the addictive mind will have periods of wishing to end the cycle, usually following a down period. However the mind is up and down, and usually to extremes, during addictive cycles.

One evening, Paul came in to my room with some printed emails, from an address name along the lines of the *Pink Rabbits*. One of his identities mentioned previously, in his ploy to create a new world-order based on peace. His creative nature and will to succeed was impressive, he had many good ideas and did actually put some into practice when we got out, such as arranging live music and other charity events. Another character called Drew arrived, a couple of days after Paul. He was the opposite in nature to Paul, not placid and kind, but very erratic and bullish, although when you got to know him he was alright and you could see his qualities, someone that would be there for his friends and quite a likable, funny guy.

Drew had been in the ward a lot and quite recently too, given his familiarity with others in there and the staff. He was a really tall stocky bloke, worked in the building industry, probably a labourer, but he may have been a tradesman. He was clever and he was obsessed with the name on the rizzla packet (the cigarette papers). He had something in common with Paul, Henry and me then, he focused a lot of his energy on symbolism and coincidences. Paul and Drew got on very well. I was starting at this point to try and not focus on coincidental symbolism for reasons explained earlier and kept my opinions to myself.

Drew had a habit of saying 'I-C-E', whilst bending his back slightly, spreading his arms out and leaning forward at the same time. It was quite inspiring actually, when you felt his positive vibes, and it was good fun to pull the same move. We had some laughs in-between dealing with his aggressive mood swings.

Pink rabbits and Ice kept themselves entertained and I turned my attention on getting out, not escaping this time, but proving to the doctors that I was back on track, over my cold-turkey and feeling a lot more normal. Every opportunity I had formally, and more importantly, informally, with the doctors and nurses was a show of my sanity.

When I knew they were making their informal observations for writing their notes on each of us, I made extra sure I was behaving normally and I made a point of doing normal things like watching the news, reading a book, or speaking to the other patients who were more normal. These more normal people were generally suffering less from manic behaviour and more from the other end of the scale, depression. The more I did these things, the quicker I actually did start feeling better too.

I shaved my beard off one morning and stopped wearing two pairs of trousers. Later that day, Paul and I played monopoly and finished it. We were both doing really well. I was feeling that my emotions were back, I had already felt my face redden a couple of times over that last day or so when holding new conversations with folk more able to have a conversation. Paul still just wanted to talk about his experiences. However, monopoly prevented much of that and as we were at one of the tables in the middle of the ward I did not want to be part of such talk at all. I wanted out.

29 STIRLING AND THE FREEMASONS

Later, in the smoking room I could not avoid the conversation with Paul, and gave in. I learnt a lot about his theories of the world being run by secret societies like the Freemasons and the Illuminati, and he referred to a book by David Ike. The name sounded familiar, but I don't think I knew anything about him. I had heard of the Freemasons though, my Dad spoke of them a few times when I was young and I think he may have joined at one time out of interest.

I must admit that although I didn't believe all of what Paul was telling me, some of it did ring a familiar note in the sense that although I had no names or ideas of these societies, I had believed that something behind the scenes was going on and I was quite interested in what he had to say.

I also enjoyed his company and didn't want to upset him. However, as time went by I tried again and again to get him to see things from my perspective, hoping that he may focus less on unknowns and more on getting himself better. He didn't, and eventually we grew distant. Though not intentional it was probably for the best for my recovery.

If you want to get yourself out of a certain set of situations, you need to be willing to stand on your own, and not to be afraid of being independent.

You'll probably find it comes pretty naturally, if you have been independently pushing your drink and drug needs, it's just a case of changing priorities. People with drink or drug problems actually have a really strong will. It's just a matter of changing your mind so that your will is in a positive direction, not a negative one. If you can will yourself to go through all the hassle, pain and stress of getting more drink and drugs into you, then doing the opposite is easier once you allow a little room for change.

Our minds naturally seek happiness, that's all that is happening in your head, there is no need to complicate the process with clever terminology. If you can allow some space in your mind for clarity, by just stopping for a day or two, and try to look at your life from another person's perspective, you can help yourself. Sometimes this is much easier said than done, a trigger is often required, such as a health scare for example.

Pretending you are somebody else who you are helping often works, as it's sometimes easier to help others than to help yourself. Helping others will help yourself and may help others in the early stages of their recover; best though to start with yourself first, as you can't truly help anyone else until you have first helped yourself.

Just as you can't expect others to trust you or be comfortable around you, until you can do so yourself; all that is needed is a little room for change to take place, and a little pointer in the right direction.

This room for change comes naturally by allowing your mind something else to focus on by removing the drink or drugs. Basically, you are trying to replace the getting high part with something else, this helps a great deal. Otherwise you are left with a big void that you may find difficult to fill, and quite often this empty space will be refilled with old habits or new addictions, if not filled with other healthier and *interesting* alternatives. They need to be interesting, something you want to try, say, learning to play the guitar for example; otherwise the mind will soon get bored.

The mind is like a little monkey, continuously jumping from one branch of thought to another. To point it in a healthier direction, from self-abuse to self-preservation, it only needs to realise that true happiness does not come from outside experience but from within.

More specifically, indescribable bliss happiness is what can be experienced when the mind is in it's natural state. I know this may sound like a lot of rubbish, and I do not claim to know all of the answers and neither have proof that what I tell you is true. However, the knowledge of which helped me to start to get free from addictive tendencies.

In truth, I believe that from the perspective of the drug taker or big drinker, someone who seeks to get high seeks to be happy, and this prospect of pure, intense happiness from a safe source, yourself; is a good driver to change your life around.

How? ...

Because what I am describing is ancient knowledge, passed down through the ages until the first recordings were written down thousands of years BC, in the ancient Indian language, Sanskrit, in a series of volumes known as the Upanishads. This knowledge is known as Vedanta.

There may not be conclusive proof of this bliss-full state of consciousness, yet there have been many scientific studies to prove the cognitive enhancements gained by meditation and stilling the mind naturally and regularly for short periods. The natural state of mind of pure bliss happiness is accomplished by giving the mind and body a chance to conserve energy and recover, by sitting quietly for a short period of time.

There are various aids to help you find the peaceful state of mind, aids to help your mind relax and slow the thought process. Just try and stop thinking for 30 seconds, it is near impossible. When the mind is in its natural state, when no thoughts are being imprinted on it, that is when your batteries can truly recharge. It is like cleaning up your computer hard-drive by carrying out a disk defragmentation, resetting your mind to its true state of being.

A good analogy is a cinema screen. We the viewers watch the movie being shown on the screen, we see all the various images and get lost in the film, and the pure nature of the cinema screen becomes forgotten. This is similar to the mind's natural state, when the images of thought are continually imprinted on it. The difference is the mind's natural canvas is not blank like the cinema screen. It may appear blank on the first encounter, though real awareness of it is deeper than the depth of field captured on a photograph taken on the longest possible exposure, with the smallest possible aperture. It's depth of field is beyond anything the human imagination can comprehend and more fulfilling too.

After about three weeks I was moved from Falkirk's secure ward to a less secure ward in Stirling, where it was possible to get out of the hospital grounds for a while. Paul followed about 2 weeks later. I was in Stirling for a further 2 months, but was allowed out for a few days over Christmas to stay at my auntie and uncles, in a nice little village in the Trossachs.

The change in environment from one hospital ward to another was unsettling and caused some of the psychosis symptoms to reappear after being fairly under control for a week or two. There was an old man in the ward, I say old, but he was probably only late fifties, early sixties. He appeared older, and this was, maybe, down to the wise outlook he had. So I'll refer to him as the wise old man for the sake of identification.

The wise old man was a successful business man and he had a very young, good-looking wife who came to visit him. My feelings of unease were heightened on arrival to Stirling, mainly due to an energetic young man with a serious heroin addiction, who showed me his lack of veins and explained that before he was hospitalised he was injecting into his groin as that was the only place he could find a vein. He was nice enough, but the two of us were like two male lions in a den of females, we were unintentionally winding each other up and although I was conscious of my part and trying to stay out of his way, it wasn't easy. I felt threatened and I felt that if I didn't make a show of standing my ground that he would have the better of me. He came across as a thug; although I think he was a nice enough bloke.

Who knows what I came across like; more than likely, another thug! In fact, after a couple of days another, older man left the ward on his own initiative, and feeling bad that I had a part to play in him not feeling at ease, I expressed my apologies to him before he left. He was fine about it and said he would come back in if he needed to. I asked him why he was in and he hinted that I already knew. He implied that I was very aware, and in the conversation he let me know he was a Freemason.

He was retired, and I am not sure exactly why he was in hospital, but I think he may have had a drink problem at some time. I say, at sometime, because I didn't get the impression that his problem was a 'problem', at least not at the time I met him. He seemed very much in control. So he left, and a couple of weeks later he did return.

The young man of a similar age to me had moved on at this stage and the ward was less busy in general. The wise old business man that I mentioned earlier had stayed and was seeming more and more like an insider to me, although not someone that the nurses and doctors were aware of. One night he openly showed me a crafty closing of the hand as he brought his medication up to his mouth whilst we were in line for the drug-trolley. So he wasn't taking medication, and he was letting me know.

Why? (maybe he was 'showing off', bragging?)

It was probably obvious to him by this point that I didn't take him for being a real patient. He had also let slip that he was a Freemason. I had experienced some real oneness with him. He would read his broadsheet newspaper and a few of us would be sitting in the living room watching the TV, and I would feel a mental connection to him, I got the feeling that he was reading my thoughts.

My thoughts were heavy in my head and fear was deeply rooted in me. I felt unsure of my new surroundings, the people, the nurses, the doctors and the unseen forces that I could feel; always watching, always there. It was like the door of madness was following me around and at any time I could trip and fall through it.

The old man who stayed was in the room next to mine. One morning I woke early and in a fragile state. It was between four and six o'clock. I couldn't get back to sleep and I was shaking in fear. My mind was set on doom, I was thinking that the world was going to end, that a nuclear world war was imminent, world war three. It felt like I was having a premonition. I also really thought that the man in the room next to me was reading my thoughts, and I wondered if he could hear them now.

As if to prove my belief, the old man in question came into the TV/smoking room to see if I was okay, as I sat on the floor in front of the TV, checking the news for an alert of something bad happening. Obviously there wasn't. What made me sure at the time, that he could read my thoughts or feel my negativity, was the fact that he came into the room, when it was unlikely that he heard me leave my room. Even if he did, why get up some two hours or more before breakfast just to walk into the TV room.

He managed to get me talking easily enough, I trusted him and I told him my fears. He explained that even if there was something bad going to happen that it was beyond my help and to try not to worry over it. I went back to my room and I think he went back to his.

Since these experiences I have come across two books that independently make references to the Masons and their connection to the ancient Egyptians and the science of the sun. They both describe the origin of the thirty-three degrees of Freemasonry, as being based on the thirty three vertebrae of the spine, although it is said that there are just nine ascending levels, as follows:

First, Second, Third, Ninth, Eighteenth, Thirtieth, Thirty-First, Thirty-Second and finally, Thirty-Third Degree Mason.

These nine levels, believed to be based on the Indian/Tibetan referenced energy centres, or *Chakras*, are said to also relate to the main endocrine glands from the bottom of the spine to the base of the brain. The word Chakra means wheel in the ancient Indian language Sanskrit, and each wheel, or energy centre, is said to contain a specific number of petals. There are seven Chakras and two opposing energies that flow between them, and as follows, which define the ninth degree.

From The Tutankhamun Prophecies, The Sacred Secret of the Mayas, Egyptions and Freemasons; Maurice Cotterell, p222:

Gland		**Chakra**		
Pituitary	=	Crown	1,000	petals
Pineal	=	Brow	96	petals
Thyroid	=	Throat	16	petals
Thymus	=	Heart	12	petals
Pancreas	=	Solar Plexus	10	petals
Ovaries/Testes	=	Sacral	6	petals
Adrenals	=	Base	4	petals

There is a link between the early Masons, the Egyptians, the Mayans, the ancient mystics of Tibet and India. This link is also represented within the book of revelations, in the New Testament Bible and the Knights Templar's quest for the Holy Grail (consciousness).

Favouring the modern world of science I would prefer not to focus on religion and mysticism unless it represents something enlightening that can be backed up. For the point of possible future investigation however, the link explained by Cotterell is worth sharing, refer *The Tutankhamun Prophecies,* p223.

The knowledge linking all of these societies and divinities as Cotterell explained, was regarding the number 144,000. The number supposedly comes from Indian philosophy, from adding up the number of petals within the first six chakras and multiplying it by the seventh, the crown chakra.

Certainly the mathematic history of the importance of the number 144 predates western mathematics and is founded in India. Being one of the natural numbers, it was used for counting and the first set of numbers forms a perfect pyramid. It is also the twelfth Fibonacci number and is the largest to be a square.

Fibonancci sequences, founded in ancient Indian mathematics, can be found in honey bee family trees, arrangement of leaves on a stem, an uncurling fern and the arrangement of a pine cone. The speed of light in free space, 144,000 minutes of arc per grid second, as per Bruce Cathie's works. This is linked to the mathematical representation of the endocrine glands (Chakras) mentioned above, where the number 144,000 is defined from adding up the petals of the first six chakras and multiplying the sum by the number of petals within the Pituitary (Crown) chakra (apologies for repetition).

We can recognise a glimpse of nature's code here, and come to realise how 144,000 written on their foreheads as stated in Revelation 14:1, is not an actual number of people who will come to realise God, but is in fact ANYONE who seeks the path through meditation. En*lightened* with the mathematical representation of light (144,000) written on their third eye chakra, or the Pineal gland.

The Fibonancci sequence of numbers represents a pyramid. It also creates a spiral, seen in flower heads, black holes sucking in stars, galaxies forming, etc. It is, I believe, the pattern of nature and a subject to be investigated further. It is the basis of harmonics and it is said that sound is the closet thing to the subtleties of creation. The universe is said to vibrate, to hum. It can also be seen by the naked eye too. Look into and meditate on an Indian Mandala (a circle of circles, representing the illustration of a mathematical Fibonancci sequence) long enough and it will vibrate and lead your mind to stillness, to the source of thought and creation.

'Round, like a circle in a circle, like a wheel within a wheel, never ending or beginning in an ever-spinning reel...' Bergman

The ancient mystics spoke of positive and negative energies that run up and down the spine from their energy centres, the chakras, and following sustained meditation become equal and cancel each other out.

The serpents that spiral the spine as per the Egyptian God Caduceus of Hermes and Freemasonry symbolism are meant to represent the nervous system and the negative and positive energies rising around the spinal column. Whilst the two wings represent the left and right hemispheres of the mind, above and between the wings is a small node representing the epicentre, or Pituitary gland (Crown Chakra).

When the electromagnetic energies within the body are balanced, equal and opposite, through the balancing of brain function, from continued meditation, melatonin is said to flow to the pineal gland and the mind and body become one, they function at the highest level. This level is referred to as being enlightened, 100% balanced brain function. Modern ECG experiments on long term meditators has proved this balancing of the left and right brain lobe activity to be true during meditation and remaining more balanced than non-meditators minds following practise. Eventually the coherence of the two becomes permanent.

According to Cotterell the secret weapons of the Thirty-Third Mason are telepathy and being able to practise out-of-body experiences. I am not so concerned about the out-of-body experience however, should you wish to know more, Cotterell explains how this is done in his book, referenced above. What does intrigue me is that I had the distinct feeling that I was being observed in hospital and in a way played, or toyed with, as part of some lesson to another fellow patient. The man carrying out this lesson I believe, was the guy who stayed in the room next to mine, the wise old businessman.

Previous to the morning that I suspected he was reading my thoughts, he had for some reason been trying to get me angry, in the sitting room. I have since learnt from Cotterell's *The Tutankhamun Prophecies* that there are two ways in which Mason's read minds.

The first is for two subjects to share the same space and for one subject to switch his mind off, through meditation; the second method which I believe I was being subjected to, was to amplify the output brainwaves of one of the subjects (in this case, me).

Brainwave activity can be increased through fear and anger. Mental patients, especially manic, psychotic ones; are usually consumed by fear and because of this, anger is never far away.

Where better for a Mason to train a fellow Mason? These two men even admitted that they were Masons! If it wasn't through personal experience I might discount this as ridiculous, however I actually respect that this may well be the truth and so what if it is, no harm was done. I am not angered in anyway, both men helped me get well, better than any Psychiatrist did anyway. That wasn't the fault of the Psychiatrists, in my opinion there were too many patients for any affective one to one care.

Mental health in the UK is a major problem with clearly a lack of staff compared to the amount of patients needing attention. Modern life pressures are causing a mental health epidemic.

The type of care, in my belief, is lacking holistic healing. There was too much focus on the use of medicine and not enough on psycho-analysis, again due to ever increasing waiting lists. That being said the introduction of Eastern techniques such as *Chi Gong* and other relaxation techniques was very helpful and a great step toward holistic healing. The recognition of creativity and appreciation of basic experiences was also helpful. Regular art and craft classes were held as were other basic human skill increasing activities, such as board games, table tennis, etc.

30 FEMININITY VS MASCULINITY

One of the things I experienced through my dips in and out of insanity was the feeling that I was neither man nor woman, yet soon after coming out of an episode I was feeling strongly feminine, although not in a gay, physical way. It was more a sense of the feminine part of myself being the stronger part of me and of the whole, in that state of being.

This is how I felt when on the verge of insanity – a bigger part of the whole than I normally am as my usual rational self. And further, when sane it's like you are just 'I' and when insane you are 'All', no in between. This is kind of what the Rastafarian saying 'I an I' comes from; self and Self, big 'S' being 'All' (things).

Think of it as if we are all part of the same whole, all beings, all animals, all matter; the whole universe back together as one. If everything is ultimately made of the same basic matter, then everything in the physical world is a manifestation of, an expansion of the basic matter. We'll look at this later in describing the three Gunas, an ancient Indian philosophy, that predates the similar Chinese philosophy of Yin and Yang.

Tea time again, take a break. If your head is thumping, you are probably thinking 'no wonder I went mad'. It is true – you can think too much, and too much focus on a subject you cannot fathom is dangerous territory for the mind. It needs stillness and rest, and thoughts should be natural, from their source, like small ripples appearing gently on the surface and coming to the shore slowly. When thought ripples become waves, they come quicker and fiercer, and like dropping a stone in the ocean, the waves go outwards in every direction. Thoughts are like this. Take a break.

Thoughts have a source, like everything does. I believe that the source is an infinite reservoir of knowledge, and that this state is experienced as pure bliss happiness: the cinema screen before the projected thought is imprinted on it. That, then, would suggest that the mind's natural state is the same as it's source of thought.

The thought comes from the source and is imprinted on the mind's screen. The natural state of the mind IS the source of thought, i.e. in it's natural state it already is aware of all thought, all things and everything that could possibly be imagined, has been imagined, has ever happened or still has come to be; it is ALL within. The Rastafarian's enlightening saying that I mentioned earlier, 'I an I', enables everyday understanding of this theory: You and me are the 'I', the All is the other I. Or think of it as conscious and subconscious, the 'Id' for the Freudian psychologists among you.

Tea break two, please. I don't want to inflict mania on you! I am not saying that your mind is too weak to take this in, quite the opposite, everyone's mind can easily pick this up, because truths are easily identified, the problem is everyone will identify in their own personal way and the monkey in our heads will branch-hop quicker than normal without control, unless you hold it back, and as yet I have not given you the tools for control.

Madness is real. I don't want to lose you before I can safely enlighten you. However, a little interest is a good thing before you meditate. In fact, some of us need that driver in the first instance. It's kind of like going to the gym. After a while it becomes routine and you enjoy the good feelings of having more energy, loose but supple muscular movement, a fitter body, etc.

However, when you go for your first run, it can be hard to keep motivated, why change your usual habits just because someone told you it can be good for you? Exactly, you need to experience it for yourself, and you need some motivation in starting.

Take that break, if you haven't already, I've had to have several in getting these points over.

The psychologist Abraham Maslow in The Farther Reaches of Human Nature explains the battle between the sexes within the individual mind quite clearly and a little crudely but it is true. He notes that there is evidence available that suggests that the sexual hormones produce not only sexual but also dominance desires.

Dominance-subordination is a fundamental differentiator for where we find ourselves on the scale of predominant female / male behaviour patterns. It is a major player in all of our relationships, with both sexes. Maslow explains that for us to get on with the other sex, we need to respect our inner opposite, then we can appreciate their qualities far more, once we have appreciated them in ourselves. This works for all relationships because everyone contains a blend of both female and male dominant behaviour which at various points in life may be required in greater forms.

The appreciation of the qualities of the opposite sex is usually overwhelming when truly realised, for example the man that becomes aware of his femininity and more importantly accepts it openly, will notice how much better these qualities are in a woman. It is beyond my intelligence and rationale but from experience I have a strong suspicion that woman are much better placed to raise themselves to transcendence and enlightenment. Their natural qualities of fantasy / dreaminess, emotional reflection is stronger than in men.

These qualities represent our creative nature. Artists will have them naturally as primary cognitive responses to thoughts that appear on their minds.

Whereas Engineers / Scientists will probably transform their pure thoughts into methodical ideas, creating feelings that will lead to an analytical representation of their thoughts.

So, there may be a deeper meaning to the term Mother Earth, something to ponder just now anyway, and look at from a more in-depth analysis later, once you have completed my journey back to reality and understood the makeup of the physical world from the point of view of the three gunas. I'll also go through a safe method of controlling the little monkey in your head.

A way of finding meditation, a technique called 'the Mindfulness of breathing', a free and easy way to settle your mind, which increases energy and thought coherence.

31 BACK TO REALITY

When I was living the story you are reading I was not aware of how to find the meditative state. I had an interest and an idea that it was a state of mind where no thoughts were there, but I didn't really understand. You may have picked this book up knowing a little of meditation and be at the same stage I was.

This is another reason for me taking you through it in this way, so that you can see the transition as I did, yet without trying to understand via your mind alone, as I did.

Don't do that please.

Have patience, we're nearly there anyway and I thank you for your patient approach and for listening to my silly stories!

You may already have plenty of knowledge and experience of meditation and what I am hinting toward. Hopefully this story rings a bell of similarity, a similar resonance ringing through your being. Maybe like me you need a helpful reminder now and then.

So we're all on the same page, (pun intended). Are you ready for the fun part?

Good. I've talked enough already and now it's time for some interaction.

I'd like you to read the following then try it: Close your eyes (not now! – wait until you read the end of the paragraph, haha).

Breathe in and out normally and say the number '1' to yourself in your mind, after you have exhaled; then breath in again and after exhaling the second time say '2', and do this for a count of 5 and then stop. Now quickly, so you notice the difference, I want you to say '1' in your mind before you inhale, then breath out, then '2', and breathe in again.

Did you notice how this feels different?

If not, try it again without stopping to read instructions, now that you know what to do. You may have noticed that the period that you count, between the breaths, is the same?

You are right, but it feels very different doesn't it?

This is your first lesson in the mindfulness of breathing.

I was a week or two into my stay in Stirling hospital when normal reality was becoming the norm again. I had settled into my new surroundings and got to know the new faces. I was probably at the stage that I was at before I left Falkirk. I had stopped using the girl's toilets that, on the occasion when I was verging on insanity and feeling feminine, had felt like the right thing to do! I was eating well again, three hot meals a day and putting weight back on. In fact, I was looking good and feeling good.

PART 3 - REHABILITATION

32 CHI GONG

There were activities during the day in the hospital ward, not compulsory, but recommended, and they certainly helped me. Before I learnt the word pranayama, the Indian art of increasing prana through breathing, I was vaguely familiar with the Chinese term *Chi*, meaning energy, life-force. Chi Gong, if you haven't heard, is a form of exercise that is supposed to open the flow of Chi within our bodies, like Thai Chi and Yoga.

The theory is that energy blockages occur within our bodies, and these can cause muscular tension and stress, physically and mentally. By carrying out some regular stretches, combined with breathing exercises to compliment them, the body can be opened to fresh, revitalising Chi. It helped me that much, that I still do a form of the exercise every morning, combined with a few favourite Yoga exercises learnt after this event. If I forget, or don't find the time to do them, I feel the tension returning to my body, mainly in the neck and shoulders where we many of us hold much of our physical stress.

When I arrived in Stirling I experienced intense pain in my neck and shoulders one evening whilst placing myself in the living/smoking room for too long where the environment was stressful. Someone advised me to take myself away from the stress and be on my own, but I wasn't used to the freedom to do this because, in Falkirk you were rarely allowed to your room, except for occasionally after dinner before the drug-trolley and bed.

Whilst on the topic of Chi, I'd like to share two experiences that help me visualise the life-force. I'm not proud of the cause of these experiences, on both occasions I was heavily sedated on cannabis. The first time I experienced it was in the school canteen. A few of us, who smoked on the way into school at the back of the bus, would go to the canteen in the morning and spend the majority of our lunch money, if we had any left after buying cigarettes, to buy munchies and straighten ourselves out after a mornings smoking session. Near the till was a small square table and we always used to stand there. Behind us was a set of double doors, and at the end of the canteen queue was another set of double doors, at the opposite end of the room. These led to the toilets.

One morning, whilst quietly eating my cake and listening to the others - I rarely spoke when stoned and turned introvert - I looked across the canteen to everyone sitting at the tables and I looked out of the window. It was a slightly grey day, but not dull. Almost as soon as I looked out of the window I became aware of a vibration in the air. The air seemed to become visible from where I stood to the window and beyond. Tiny particles of clear, or white light appeared to bounce off each other in every direction. It was dense and it was everywhere I looked. Nauseous with fear that I was hallucinating, something not usually experienced with smoking weed, I made my way along the length of the canteen whilst holding onto the wooden rail that separated the queue, to guide me in a straight line to the toilets.

Fortunately, no one was in the toilet and I splashed cold water over my face. It worked and I could no longer see the air vibrating around me. The bell rang and I made my way cautiously to registration. I sat in my usual seat and did not look out of the window, I stared straight ahead and gathered my remaining wits to appear calm and collected.

The second time I experienced the same phenomena I was at a friend's home near Liverpool. I was on a two-week holiday, back from Barbados, and had spent the night drinking and taking a small amount of cocaine. My friend didn't take drugs, but he was okay with me doing it. I rolled a joint of strong 'skunk' cannabis weed and went out in his garden to smoke it. He went to bed and I sat on his paving slabs with my back to the outside wall of his house. His garden was really green, lots of grass and surrounded by trees with thick foliage. It was summer and the early morning light was very similar to the day that I experienced the event previously, at school.

All of a sudden I looked up from smoking and everywhere I looked, the air, the trees, the grass, everything was made of bouncing particles. I could view them individually, like Scottish midges, but they bounced off each other in every direction and vibrated. It was a beautiful pattern. This time I didn't freak out because I was on my own and with no immediate danger of being caught taking drugs. I watched for ages. My head was too mashed to contemplate what it was, but it certainly didn't feel like a hallucination.

I've experienced hallucinations with LSD and ecstasy, and although they are often believable and as real as day, this was even more real-like. It was more a sense of my eyes had adjusted or been brought to the attention of it. It was as if it always happens and only now I could actually see it with my eyes.

I do, in fact, crazy as this sounds, believe there to be some truth in this, although I cannot remember what I knew back then, about Chi or life-force. I was aware that this was energy and that it made up everything that I could see. It surrounded everything, it was everything, and it was beautiful, it was also alive. How else could it vibrate and permeate everything.

33 LOCH KATRINE

Some Chi Gong sessions later, a day on the beers in Stirling with a fellow patient where we both got piercings, and then a few days release to spend Christmas with my relations in Perthshire. I eventually get full release two or three weeks into January 2004. I was off the drugs, and the mania was under control. However, my spirit was low, I think the reality that I had lost my career and place in society hit me with the cumulative effect of taking regular anti-psychotics, and this had made me depressed.

My auntie and uncle kindly put me up in their house. My youngest cousin was at home at the time and going through the process of applying to attend university. At the time he was working at the local short bread factory and was totally fed up with it.

During the day I was on my own, whilst everyone was at work. You may think this would be great, but I had spent my time working, from the age of sixteen, straight from school. I was not used to sitting about. I fell into a pattern of reading late and waking late. With no one or nothing to get me out of bed, day turned into night, at least for the mornings. When I did get up I used my time to write letters to my uncle Frank. I was determined to understand my experiences and although Frank informed me that he did not call the birds, he did not leave his body to give me a message in Barbados or anything like that, he was however, amazed with how my subconscious had unfolded to get me back to Scotland.

Frank is a clever guy, more than clever he has a profound awareness of life, and our letter-writing helped me articulate my jumbled thoughts and give some rational meaning to them and to my experiences. In the very least I was able to label some of my experiences and understand what had happened. Whilst in Falkirk hospital I drafted the structure of this book, just raw chapter headings, twelve in total. They haven't changed either, just expanded to more chapters, to break it up a bit and make the reading, hopefully, easier. Anyway, I tell you this because the very action of drafting this book by a series of journals over the years, has been a serious and most definite therapy for me.

My friend Dan from the states, who I met whilst sailing in Barbados, suffered from mental illness when he was younger, and when we met he was studying psychology and philosophy. He now has his own business and is a Yoga teacher and therapist. He used to keep a journal too, it was a way for him to understand his subconscious mind and the reasons for continuing with negative habits and choices. You see by becoming aware of the source of our negative tendencies we can break them.

This reminds me of a saying of Henry's, in Falkirk hospital, it went along the lines of, 'Accentuate the positive, minimise the negative'. Again, it is the field of opposites. You cannot remain in one area, but you can be open to the change and grasp it when it comes. What I mean is, if you are feeling positive, be careful and do not let things run away with themselves, if you get too giddy you aim to fall quicker and lower. Like a bad hangover, the heavier the night before, the worse the symptoms.

Now if you are feeling negative, would the theory be the same? Of course. After feeling extremely negative, you may spike into positivity abruptly with little control of the duration. Remember that at opposite ends of the scale the results may be similar, but understanding their passing can be difficult, especially if your natural nature is at the opposite end of the scale, and you want to know how to control the short term dip or rise in the other. It is like being a man, trying to understand a woman, or vice versa. Essentially we are both human beings with similar core needs, food, water, shelter, heat, sex, a feeling of being useful, loved and wanted; but put yourself in the mind of the opposite sex. Can you easily understand how they think and seek to fulfil their needs? No, me neither, and I count myself as better than average.

So if you feel negative, all you need do is tell yourself that no state of mind sticks forever, try not to dwell on the negativity any more than you feel is necessary and be open to a change in mood. When the change arrives, as it always will, be prepared for it and embrace it. When you are in your positive place, control the intensity, hold the reins back tight enough so that you keep moving in positivity, but not too tight that you stop the flow altogether. It's a balance and it's easier to experience through regular meditation, Chi Gong, Thai Chi or Yoga, than it is to just will your mind through visualisation.

What a lot of people tend to do when they get a positive break, if they have been feeling extremely negative, is go on a mental shopping trip to the most expensive, extravagant, designer shops and spend it all at once. Then before you know it, it's back to long days and nights of feeling down and helpless. Don't waste your chance to create more positive space, this space will gradually deepen and become more natural to reside in than the darker places you have been residing in of late.

So I started this book and wrote letters to my uncle every week, and he replied as quickly. The process accelerated my understanding and acceptance of what had happened. The majority of the books I refer to throughout were brought to my attention through my uncle Frank. By reading these, plus a few others, it enabled me to put my experiences into words.

During three months of doing some writing, reading, and thinking, and a lot of eating and sleeping, I started trying the mindfulness of breathing technique. I got some instant benefits, but my mind was restless and I struggled to get into a daily routine. I was depressed, not deeply, but deep enough that I couldn't snap out of it. The daily boredom had me applying for jobs that I would not usually consider and I even tried to get back to Barbados, but fortunately my old boss told me that my position had been taken.

I took a good, local job in the end, to break my negative cycle, as a bike-hire assistant on the banks of Loch Katrine, in the Trossachs. It was a summer job from April until September.

34 CHANGE YOUR MIND

Your breath is the safest route to peace and bliss-consciousness. Why is a route other than this not safe, you may ask? Well, there are other ways to reach the fourth state of consciousness, such as through the use of a mantra, but this requires having a teacher.

There are a certain set of safe mantras, which are Sanskrit words, or sounds, that are suited to your personality, if you like. For example, did you know that improper use of the mantra 'Om' can tend to make people recluse? I'm going to stop this topic now as we are not doing mantra, however, before I give you the mindfulness of breathing technique let's consider the pros and cons of meditating.

Personally, I think that there is no con, it's all positive and from the start you experience positive results. Everyone has a different level of result at the beginning, with some experiencing little, some more, but eventually it takes us all to the same place anyway.

I now believe in responsible action and therefore I am of the nature to explain some of the results I have experienced.

Meditation has turned my life around full-circle. Not changed me as such, I am still the same, but I am more aware of who I am, and of what makes me react. It has helped me foresee my reaction to situations, to other people's negativity, for example, that was previously sometimes an excuse for my drunkenness and drug abuse.

With understanding comes control of mind and subsequently control of physical actions. However, it is only fair to explain that occasionally this also brings some pain. Not the kind of pain discussed earlier where I was unable to focus my mind, that pain, although mental, had a personal or physical edge to it, like someone was injecting my mind with long thick needles. The pain I talk of now is nowhere near intense, it is infrequent and easily controlled, but it is unavoidable; it equates from two things.

One, is the realisation that your past actions caused suffering to others; the other is interaction with others whom are unaware of the result of their actions.

The first I think you can easily understand, we all do things we regret. This is more easily resolved, because if you feel real remorse and regret then you have reached a higher level of thinking and you can let yourself be free of whatever has pained you. Why?

Because you have changed your behaviour. Yes, that's right, change is possible whilst still keeping your positive attitude, providing that you truly have realised the errors of your ways.

The latter result is out of your control and this is where stress can arise. I think of it as developing myself, always striving to understand what makes me react. When you understand whatever is stressing you out, you no longer see it as a problem. Maybe not one hundred percent of the time because we are human and not always in the best frame of mind.

Now knowing that others around you are sometimes acting out of ignorance makes it possible for you to overlook actions and forgive. However, it can be painful to you knowing that you could help, but you are helpless. These other people do not need to be directly close or related to you to affect you, but by some connection you are involved. The closer the connection the more emotionally difficult it is to approach them without conflict because you know that the other person will not become aware of the full picture just through explanation.

The further attached the connection the more difficult the communication resides in the fact that the other person will not know you well enough to take your comments to heart. And again, even if they do, they won't be as fully aware of the situation as you are.

Wisdom can bring such a thorn in our sides. The choice of what to say and when to say it, if at all, automatically defaults to the wisest of the companions. It isn't easy standing by watching situations unfold, no matter how much it is realised that they have to be. Also it is not about intelligence, or basic common sense, but a general awareness of our own emotions, and from that level, an understanding of how other people's emotions and auto-responses affect their actions.

Despite the above, I believe on the whole it is better to be more aware. I certainly have less personal problems and more control of my life than I did before. When I ask myself what is better, being the person entangled in stressful situations or the onlooker, the answer is definitely to be the onlooker. Even if sometimes there can be what feels like important choices to make that otherwise you would not have had to concern yourself with. Of course, the onlooker can easily become one of those entangled if the wrong choices are made, or the right ones at the inappropriate time.

Being truly wise is helping without being caught up in the emotion. Being humble is helping without others realising, and not seeking thanks or gratitude. I realise I'm drifting here, but if you have caught my drift then I can move on with the knowledge that I have tried to be responsible for warning you of the effects of gaining awareness.

Gaining awareness is a side-effect of meditation. People practice meditation for different reasons; some to seek greater awareness, but others for physical and mental well being. Relaxation is another name for meditation. Most people who go to Yoga or marshal arts classes will do some form of relaxation and there are various different types of Yoga and other relaxation therapies around.

The meditation technique, or more accurately the technique of relaxation that leads to a meditative state that I am about to teach you, comes from a Buddhist called Paramananda.

The book, Change Your Mind, by Paramananda was given to me by a close friend whom I met in Barbados. She came to visit me in hospital in Stirling and we went for coffee. At this stage I was allowed out during the day for as long as I liked and it was good to be semi-free.

A couple of weeks later I arranged to get the train from Stirling to Glasgow. I was a little nervous to be travelling again, especially by train. My friend met me at Queen Street station and we had coffee at the platform café. This is when she gave me the aforementioned book, and another on Shiatsu. You may remember the sailing trip to Bequia, well this is the same friend, who had told me about Shiatsu.

At the platform café, pigeons were accumulating around us. It felt too eerie, and I had the feeling we were being watched, so we left and walked through town a little while before going to a bar for some lunch.

Afterwards, we went to another bar and I had a pint of Guinness. I had been having a couple of drinks again, but trying to stay sober. It was kind-of working and I seemed better at staying in control than usual, but I knew that I was on borrowed time. Still, you can borrow time for as long as you desire, what you have to give back is where you have to be careful. Something called Karma, or whatever you want to call it, trust me it is real.

It is unadvisable to sail along doing what you like without thinking of your actions - what kind of actions are they, could they be better? Should you be doing it at all, what risk are you putting yourself and others in? These kinds of questions are good to ponder if you want a life less stressful and more meaningful.

So we talked a while and remembered times in Barbados, and then I thanked her again for the books and her kindness, and she thanked me for looking out for her in Barbados, and then I got the train back to Stirling.

On the train the hangover from a couple of drinks kicked in and I felt a bit paranoid. All of a sudden I was on the edge of insanity again. I used some breathing exercises I learnt during the Chi Gong practice, and went straight to chapter two in Change Your Mind, after browsing the contents. The first exercise helped a great deal and I resumed control of my thoughts. I rode the 'anxiety carriage' back to Stirling and by the time I walked the two miles back to hospital, I was back to normal.

It was dark when I got in, but not because it was late, it was Winter. I had missed dinner, but I was in time for some supper, which I had after taking my medication, and then I went to bed early to sleep off the alcohol.

I was looking forward to reading the book, Change Your Mind, and I had high hopes of learning meditation with it because I trusted my friend's knowledge of Shiatsu, which I believed was somehow related. She had been recommended the book by a close friend, a Buddhist monk whom she had known for years, from a mountain loch-side retreat in central Scotland.

Are you ready for the gift of a lifetime then? I recommend you buy the book for an in depth account and more information on development, such as a chapter called Insight. The following is my recollection of the practise in my own words and what I practised for about ten years before changing to Transcendental Meditation (TM).

Starting with sitting posture, this is not so important to start with as your body will naturally find the right posture as you get used to the practise, but try and sit cross-legged if comfortable, keep your back straight and imagine someone has a piece of string tied to your head pulling it upwards toward the ceiling or sky.

It is probably best to sit on a cushion or two, as this helps to keep your back straight and eases any strain at the bottom of your back. Let your crossed legs rest on the ground. Look straight ahead, but you can let your head tilt ever so slightly downward toward your chest, think of this as keeping your heart in mind. Close your eyes gently, relax your shoulders and face muscles and let your eyes rest about twelve inches in front of you, just far enough away that your eyes are not straining and not trying to cross focus.

Stop just now and try it. Sit on a cushion with your back straight, legs crossed, looking straight ahead about twelve inches in front of you and then gently close your eyes. By the way, the visual area of about twelve inches directly ahead of you is focussing some awareness on this area of your mind that deals with 'seeing', with vision, even if your eyes are closed.

The part of the brain between and above the eyes is known as your third eye, a chakra. Not important just now, we'll come to chakras later, and sight. It is not uncommon though to experience visions, not like dreams as such, but more often light. This is normal, and if you experience these kinds of things it will be pleasant, so there is no need to fret. Any visions, thoughts or other experience is just stress release and should not be focused on.

You are ready to learn the breathing now, here we go.

<u>Step 1</u>: Sitting in your comfortable position, become aware of your breath as it enters your body, close your mouth and let your nose do the breathing (if you don't have a cold that is, because breathing through the nose is more subtly experienced).

After two or three breaths, say the number '1' to yourself, in your head, following exhalation. Never force the breath, you are becoming aware of it, not trying to control it, just breathe naturally.

After exhaling and saying one to yourself, breath in again, then out, and then say the number two, then in and exhale again, number three; do this up to a count of ten and then start again at one, and so on. Do this for about three to five minutes.

To start with you can use a clock or a timer and open one eye quickly to check if need be, after a while though you won't need to, and timing is not so important as long as you are focussed on the stage you are at before going into the next stage.

<u>Step 2:</u> Stop counting for a breath or two and just follow the breath as it enters your body and leaves it. Then say the number one in your mind before you inhale through your nose, it is exactly the same point at which you said the number before (between breaths), but it feels very different. Breath out, say number '2' then inhale, breathe out, number '3' then inhale, and so on up to ten. Again, repeat for three to five minutes.

Don't worry if you end up counting to 50! It's natural for your mind to wander and think of things, just gently bring it back to the counting and start at number one in whatever stage you are in. If you are really struggling in step two, you maybe went into it too quickly, don't fight your thoughts, just start back at step one again. If you try it again and you are still struggling, or don't have much time, or getting stiff from sitting too long, then carry on through the practise and next time you sit to meditate it might be easier.

Step 3: When you are ready, drop the counting and continue to breathe as you were, following your breath from the point that you felt it reach the tip of your nose, and in through to your chest, then down into your abdomen, and then follow it out. Again, repeat for three to five minutes.

Just observe your breath, be aware of it, do not try and alter it. If your mind wanders as you try to concentrate on your breathing, gently bring it back to the breath. This is being mindful of your breathing.

Your body should now be naturally relaxed; your face muscles relaxed, your shoulders relaxed and hopefully your posture is still good. It is okay to fall asleep, if you are tired don't fight it, have a sleep and if you have time start at step 1 again when you wake up.

Step 4:
Now for the final step, a minor alteration to step 3 - **just focus on the area where your breath enters and exits your body (usually the tip of your nose). Do this for three to five minutes, or as long as you like.**

Total length of practise can vary from ten to thirty minutes, I suggest when you start, don't try and do any more than thirty minutes and aim for twenty. You probably will not be used to sitting in this position for so long. Twenty minutes is a good target and duration. Remember, steps 1 to 3 are just breathing exercises (as is step 4) and trying to get you into a meditative state. Not every sitting will get you into this state, and it could take days, weeks, or months; depending on how often you do it (I suggest twice a day).

In the morning try to sit before you eat or drink, as your metabolism will be working to digest what you have consumed. Try to go to the toilet beforehand, for similar reasons. In the afternoon or evening aim for the same and don't meditate right before bed as you will be too alert to sleep. However just doing step one is a good way to get to sleep, imagine all the stress leaving with every out-breath.

You can do steps 1 to 3 on public transport, sitting in the passenger seat of a car, or walking, almost anywhere. But, be advised not to do it at work or when driving, in charge of machinery, etc.

If you need energy and confidence do step 2 and imagine pure white light entering your body and going down into your abdomen (your centre and reserve of energy).

You can also imagine a golden bowl in your abdomen, gradually filling with the white light that enters in and out of your body. Never force, always naturally. I read this in my friend's Shiatsu book and tried it a couple of times. It works, but it's not something I do regularly (or, on a regular basis).

When doing the mindfulness of breathing technique, steps 1 to 4 above, there is little point in doing visualisation, your goal is not to think (to transcend thought), and visualising is a form of thinking. Your aim is to focus on the breath and that alone, it is just a tool to help slow your thoughts and reach meditation.

Don't do it in the dark, a little light is fine.

I am not going to tell you what to expect, as I never knew and I don't want to disappoint you if you have a different experience. However, I will say that after practise it is normal for your breathing to refine itself so that you could actually believe you are not breathing anymore, it is that subtle. If this happens I don't need to say not to panic because this will only happen if you are on the verge of transcending, and therefore it will feel right and your awareness will keep any fears at bay.

Trust me, oxygen is still getting to your brain, it's just that your body is in a state of energy conservation and, in fact, is gaining immense benefit from allowing prana (Chi, life-force) to flow all around your body. There is no fear of any kind when near this state of being; you will be confidently aware in silent bliss. Awareness of this and everything else that comes from this is unexplainable in words and so you have to experience it yourself to understand.

35 BHAGAVAD GITA

During my time working at the cycle hire in the Scottish tourist destination, the Trossachs, there were many days leading up to the summer that were very quiet, especially in April and May. Some of these quiet days were spent doing other jobs like painting fences, but most of the time was spent sitting in the steel container that stored the bikes, sat on a bucket awaiting customers.

One of the ways I passed my day was reading and at this time I was reading a translation of the Bhagavad-Gita by Maharishi Mahesh Yogi, the founder of the Transcendental Meditation Technique.

This book was recommended to me by my uncle Frank, following our recent letter communications, as he believed some of the theories and experiences I was expressing were better understood by reading this. The Bhagavad-Gita itself is an ancient scripture from India, written down in the ancient Sanskrit language approximately 200 years BC. It is an account of a conversation between Arjuna, a warrior and famous archer and Lord Krishna.

Although I am not a religious person I was at the time basing a lot of my experiences on religious ideas, because they were the closest thing I was familiar with to relate to. However the Transcendental Meditation programme is not a religious one, it is based on scientific principles and backs-up the personal results of regular meditation through scientific analysis, such as increased cognitive coherence that has been measured in analysing the pattern of brain waves before, during and after meditation.

The translation is not religious based either, and is written in a very systematic and clear way that is relatively easy to follow. The main point of the story is to show how the Lord Krishna raised Arjuna's awareness through conversation by giving Arjuna the technique for Self-realisation. Arjuna was in conflict with himself, as a Warrior he had a duty to uphold the law and do good, the people he was being forced to fight were related to him and he was unsure what to do.

The most important verse in the whole text is Verse 45, Chapter 2

Chapter 2, Verse 45: **The Veda's concern is with the three gunas. Be without the three gunas, O Arjuna, freed from duality, ever firm in purity, independent of possessions, possessed of the Self.**

In his translation and commentary Maharishi explains how Krishna, with very few words has given Arjuna the ability to be free from the forces of opposites that constitute the whole of relative existence. As I explained earlier everything has an opposite, and until you transcend this relative field of opposites you are exposed to the pulling and pushing of them.

The Three Gunas are like ***Yin and Yang***. In fact, it is most probable that Yin and Yang derived from the Gunas, because I think ancient Indian philosophy predates Chinese philosophy. The theory is similar in that there are two opposing forces but the third force balances the two opposites. The Vedas is the name of the volumes that contain the knowledge of relativity, the knowledge of existence, the meaning of life and creation. The Three Gunas are at the heart of that knowledge, because for every living organism on earth, be it plant, animal or human being each and every guna is present in varying ratios. One cannot be present without the other two.

The names and natures of the gunas are Sattva, creative; Tamas, destructive; and Rajas, activity. The entire creation is said to consist of the interplay of these three forces and evolution is creation with progressive development. Rajo-guna provides the activity to create a spur, whilst sato-guna and tamo-guna are needed to uphold the direction of the movement. This can be realised through the following example, a plant grows through a spur of rajas activity, rain and sunlight and the nutrients in the soil spur the seed to sprout roots and leaves. Sattva plays it's part in this creation and then for the creation sequence to re-start a Tamas destructive process is first required where the plants wilt, die and re-fertilise the soil; all aspects of evolution can be viewed in such a way.

For those Star Wars lovers out there you may begin to note the similarities, Lord Veda, Yoda (Yoga), etc. Before enlightenment one becomes aware of the finer aspects of nature, of the Vedas. Upon enlightenment, one becomes master of the Vedas, like Master Jedi, Lord Veda, although veda is not bad like Darth Veda, that was his name because he was deemed to be a master of the forces of nature. It is likely that one can learn to control the forces of nature before enlightenment and therefore be not entirely good in nature; but to become truly enlightened is only to be pure in nature and therefore all good. In this state all action is good action.

The Vedas were passed down through the ages by song, through rhymes and hymns and then around 5000 years BC they were recorded in written Sanskrit volumes, known as the Upanishads. They contain all the knowledge and wisdom of the ages passed, you would be amazed how intellectual they are; for example they contain simple ways of carrying out complicated trigonometry and arithmetic.

The ancients charted the stars, they knew how to calculate huge distances between planets and, if I am not mistaken, the ancient Indian wisdom is the source of astrology, Vedic Astrology, Vedic Mathematics. Some searching on the internet provides great research into this.

When I was younger I was in conflict with myself over the truth of astrology, now I believe the art is real when practised correctly. It can tell us much about our personalities. This is another direction that leads to the same truths and something I do not know enough about to discuss further, but it does interest me greatly. I may mention a famous name before I move on, Jonathan Cainer, he certainly respects the old wisdom of the East. I believe he follows the western rules of astrology that differ only marginally as discussed. His daily forecasts are really accurate and he also has very wise thoughts of the day on his web page, www.cainer.com.

Getting back to Verse 45, the Vedas concern is with the three gunas, i.e. the Vedas are the rules of life and they require the three gunas for the rules to work. To understand the Vedas all one needs to do is transcend them, through meditation. At this level of awareness the pure knowledge of life is easily understood. Krishna is providing a different approach. Modern psychology these days is to find the causes of effects.

However, this way is to introduce a second element to influence the first. Hence he is saying 'Be without the three gunas', which means stop acting, stop thinking and just be. This is known as Being, the nature of this state of being is pure bliss happiness, transcendental consciousness, an unlimited source of energy, wisdom, and peace.

It should be noted that the state of Being is the source of all thought and action and hence by introducing a second element he is also investigating the cause in order to influence the effect.

The greatness of Lord Krishna's teaching lies in its direct practical approach and its completeness from every point of view. The idea of introducing a second element and the idea of investigating the cause in order to influence its effect represent two principles distinctly opposed to each other, yet both of them are fulfilled in one technique. It is this completeness of practical wisdom that has made the Bhagavad-Gita immortal . Maharishi Mahesh Yogi.

From my own point of view, any text that contains such extensive wisdom in such few words, such as Verse 45, is worthy of respect.

The next part of the verse, **'*Freed from duality, ever firm in purity*'**, is a natural by-product of the state of Being.

Duality fails to be when relative existence is transcended. This is because there are no actions taking place, no thoughts or desires to produce actions, no cause for duality.

This state in its very nature is purity and therefore if someone is in this state of being then they are ever firm in purity. In Indian philosophy there are seven states of consciousness, described as follows.

The first three states are sleeping, dreaming and waking and are experienced daily. The fourth state is known as Pure Consciousness. This is the state of Being we are learning about. However to describe it is like trying to describe the taste of a strawberry, you can't, you can only eat it to get the nourishment and pleasure of it.

The nature of being is simply bliss, without any activity, of thought or otherwise. It is through experience of that pure consciousness that the intellect, mind, learns to accept that it is un-describable and get on with its real work in the relative.

Pure consciousness, or being, is the source of thought. To try and describe it with language born of thought, creates a paradox and if you are not careful it can cause your mind to fall into madness, which was part of my problem. I had a deep desire to understand this state, thinking that I could grasp it with my mind. It is not of the mind, it is the essential nature of the mind. Although it is an infinite source of wisdom and energy, the intellectual wisdom comes through experience and the intellectual consideration of that experience.

Consciousness has to be experienced it cannot be understood by the intellect alone, it is like the computer describing the programmer and the reason why it was programmed. To dive into consciousness regularly through meditation and come out again to experience the relative field of life that we know normally, provides a better understanding and greater wisdom becomes of it.

Awareness of what makes you stressed, negative and unhappy, this all comes from regular meditation and enables you to deal with it better and avoid it in the future. It also creates a better tolerance of others negativity, because you understand the similarities between yourself and everyone else.

This regular diving in and out of pure, transcendental, consciousness eventually infuses pure consciousness with everyday waking, sleeping and dreaming, and becomes **Cosmic Consciousness**, the fifth state. This is when every thought and action is in the right direction, for the good of the whole, because no matter what relative state of consciousness the person is in, they are always aware of pure consciousness and living in a blissful state of supreme awareness, all of the time.

The sixth state is known as **God Consciousness** and the final seventh state is **Unity Consciousness** or Yoga, Union. However, from my waking state and limited knowledge I personally cannot denote any differences from Cosmic Consciousness. I suspect the changes are so subtle they can only be understood from that state of being.

When I was in hospital I knew nothing of the above, it has helped me explain my experiences since though. I think drugs sometimes have a tendency to take your mind to subtle states of the Vedas and these experiences are too real sometimes to discount.

The danger is the body is not in a state of relaxation, quite the opposite, it is under intense stress and when not in a state of relaxation that only comes through regular meditation, the mind becomes anxious and fear takes over.

Apparently, it's true that we can have 'glimpses' of 'higher' states of consciousness, peak experiences, for example. But we can't maintain them with an inadequate nervous system.

In understanding the following part of the verse: *Independent of possessions, possessed of the Self*, you should be aware that there are no desires for possessions in the state of *Being* and so there are no possessions; i.e. you are independent of them, and alone, but content to be so. Because you are alone with the unbounded Self, and everything belongs to the Self.

Note the capital 'S' in *Possessed* of the *Self*, this is different to being possessed of the relative self with a small 's'. Krishna is not referring to self-obsession, vanity or self-centred thinking, but the Self as in the part of you that is your true self, without desire, conflict or anger. The *Self* can be thought of as *Being*, as *Consciousness*, unlimited wisdom, energy and life.

This Self that is referred to is similar in every being, it is the same Being. In fact, it is the home of ourselves if you like, where all come from at birth and go back to at death. We are all similar in the sense that we all originate from the same source and our essential nature is the same. It is a little crazy to think like this, but by transcending everyday, relative experience and giving it a little thought, it becomes natural to see everything as one and part of the same whole.

There is a widely-held belief that our everyday waking experience is nothing more than an illusion. However, to think like this is not healthy and will probably hinder your natural path to fulfilment. If you hurt yourself, you cannot easily stop the pain by telling yourself that it is not real.

Likewise if you have loved ones and children, you know that their existence is real, it is in your heart and evidenced by your love for them and their love for you. Illusion is not the best way to look at it, we share our world with people we love and people we do not, but we must respect them all and everything that we share our world with, all of nature in fact. Not doing so will hinder your path to inner fulfilment and realisation.

The similarities I refer to are at the core of our beings and only when we experience that subtlety will we really understand our connection with everything and everyone.

When the mind alone tries to do this it comes up with the thought that there can only be one person, one being, and that everything resides in the mind of one and therefore everyone and everything else is a mere illusion, this is the product of madness and let me explain from my personal experience of it, that madness is all it is (also known as Solipsism). Try not to focus the mind on things that it cannot understand. Let your awareness come naturally from meditation and reflect on what is changing in your life at the stage you are at.

Some following verses of interest from Maharishi's translation:

Chapter 2 Verse 47: You have control over action alone, never over its fruits. Live not for the fruits of action, nor attach yourself to inaction.

Chapter 2 Verse 48: Established in Yoga, O winner of wealth, perform actions having abandoned attachment and having become balanced in success and failure, for balance of mind is called Yoga.

36 RELAPSE

The summer ended and so did my contract at Loch Katrine cycle-hire. It had been a good summer and I had met some new friends. On my birthday, in late August, we went to Glasgow to re-visit my favourite club, and having not been that long since my party days, I still had a contact to score ecstasy, and that's what I did.

Don't ask me why, other than old habits and memories of happy high-times that die-hard. Although I had started trying to meditate it was infrequent and I was still seeking happiness externally.

I was smoking weed and drinking again, although much less than before hospital, and was keeping in control. Then I started another job, in the shortbread factory where my cousin had worked.

Every Friday the factory closed at midday and most workers would go to the local pub. This was crazy because we never earned enough money to piss it up the wall the day after pay day, but that's what most of us did. Some had sense to go home after one or two drinks. Not me of course, I was still out at last orders, which in Scottish villages can be as late as 1:30am, then possibly a party, or round to a mate's for a smoke.

Unfortunately, the unhappiness of working on the production line all day from 7:30am until 5:30am, with two half-hour breaks, to get some day light and fresh air, was sucking the life out of me. It was good for me though, it made me respect and be grateful for the opportunities I had wasted.

The factory work was boring and it was no wonder that the workforce changed regularly, although some young lads had been there since leaving school. It had become the norm for them and they had their different negative attitudes to the work, attitudes that I recognised. I had to break the spell before it was too late for me too. It was six months though, before I finally got a break.

There is little point going back to the stories of drunkenness and immoral behaviour, but let's just say that it was nowhere near as bad as it used to be, yet I was aware of it. I feared the pain of madness yes, but also I was aware of how my behaviour would affect others.

It was impossible to go on like that, else risk being even worse than I was before, and so I took a stand again, I stood up against that part of my mind that was set to self-destruct. I started going to AA meetings. I had been asked by fellow patients in Stirling hospital to attend with them, but I had made my excuses and avoided the meetings.

I also started reading Susan's book on alcoholism again, stopped snacking on sugar and white flour products and I started the gym. This was vitally important to my sobriety. One, because it filled a space in my life, instead of going for a drink after work on Friday as I avoided the weekly routine. Secondly, the exercise made me feel happy, as it got the endorphins in my brain working.

Finally, and equally as important, I meditated whenever I got the chance, usually after work, as the mornings were such an early start. Around this time, Chi-Gong became a daily practise for me morning and night. I had done it on and off since learning in hospital. It is said that the exercise helps energy, or

Chi (life-force) to flow more easily around the body, as previously explained.

It awakens your muscles and mind if nothing else, and increases blood flow to the brain and vital organs.

37 AA

The return to AA since my first meeting in Chester, two-and-a-half years prior, was slightly different. The first time I had almost expected a magic solution to my problem and although I was probably more of a practising Christian then, seeing as my girlfriend was a Catholic and I considered converting, having discussed marriage with her; I did make a mental note that the AA focussed a lot on a higher power and hinted toward Christianity.

The reason for this I believe is that the co-founder of Alcoholics Anonymous, Bill Wilson, from East Dorset, Vermont, USA, was introduced to the evangelical Christian Oxford Group. This group was formed by an American Christian missionary, Dr Frank Buchman, following his initial movement prior to this, called *A First Century Christian Fellowship*.

Interestingly enough, Bill Wilson stumbled upon the higher power method following a personal (Peak) Experience. Apparently, Bill met an old drinking friend, who, through the guidance of the Oxford Group, had managed to stay sober for a number of weeks. This man was Ebby Thacher and he later became the sponsor of Bill Wilson. Bill Wilson became the sponsor of the other founder, Dr Bon Smith, when realising that a major key in keeping the door of sobriety open was to help others.

This is how the fellowship began, within the Oxford Group. However it might be appreciated that Wilson was said not to be that into religion before his Peak Experience, that occurred following his fourth hospitalisation, where he was told by his doctor that if he didn't stop drinking he would die from Alcoholism or have to be locked up permanently. So during his treatment of the DTs (Delirium tremens), which is Latin for "shaking frenzy"; he was depressed, and despairingly, whilst lying in bed, he cried out, "I'll do anything! Anything at all! If there be a God, let Him show Himself!"

According to Wilson he then had the sensation of a bright light, a feeling of ecstasy and a new serenity. Now having recently found this out in researching the roots of AA, you can imagine my surprise at the interesting likeness to my sensation of bright light emanating from the bird, my feeling of ecstasy whilst sober, and my subconscious message to myself to get home, that subsequently led to my recovery.

I can also personally relate to how helping others to remain sober, can help; and likewise with other addictions or problems. Talking to others who have experienced the same or similar, can really help those people. There is a limit though, I believe, as to how much energy you can give before you actually turn the scales from helping yourself through helping others and leaving yourself withdrawn or vulnerable. The ability is learnt through experience.

Sponsorship is one of the key messages of AA, to obtain a sponsor, someone to call at anytime, when feeling a relapse is near. They may need the call as much as you need to make it. Likewise, sponsoring someone else is just as important. Another key message is to avoid the first drink and this is very much helped by having a sponsor.

It is of no surprise then that AA's other key messages result from the Christian movement, the Oxford Group, who later became a non-religious organisation, the *Initiatives of Change*, some sixty six years after the Alcoholics broke away and created Alcoholics Anonymous.

Although I've noted some failings of AA in earlier references throughout, I believe if the programme is strictly followed it can work to maintain sobriety. I remained sober whilst I was going to meetings. Refining and modernising the fellowship may be a positive suggestion however, if more alcoholics can be kept sober. It is stated that AA is not a religious or political movement, and must remain so in order to help everyone. This is true.

It is also inspiring to learn that the movement where it all began is now a non-religious movement.

Another very interesting link to AA is Carl Gustav Jung, who was already going to be a part of my story for other interesting reasons, but who has managed to pop in earlier than expected. Jung was a famous psychologist who gave society Analytical Psychology, and through his written works formed a very substantial grounding for modern psychology; not too dissimilar to the universally accepted Darwinian evolutionary theory.

Jung was the psychologist to a wealthy family, and specifically to a member who suffered alcoholism, a man named Rowland Hazard. Apparently, Jung proposed to Hazard that a *vital spiritual experience* was needed to enable a change of lifestyle, as no medicine was available for such an illness.

This link of Jung to AA came when Hazard sought out the Oxford Group and became friends with Ebby Thacher. Realisation of a global epidemic, stemming from modern living, was bringing these people together and the underlying treatment was humbly giving oneself to a higher power. This is where the serenity prayer comes in, "God grant me the serenity to accept the things I cannot change, courage to change the things I can, and wisdom to know the difference".

Again, it is of no surprise that the origin of AA is now known as the Initiatives of Change, as the serenity prayer is based on change! Either accept the fact that you are responsible for change and have the ability to do so, or accept the fact that there are factors you cannot change and learn how to deal with those. Usually the first point relates to being able to change whether you take the first drink or not; and laterally the second point often relates to a situation or person who is adding to the complicated reasons as to why one often takes a drink in the first place.

We are not ever able to change other people, they must realise their own need to change and then they might, if the environment is right for them. We should never try to change others and it is important to recognise that by trying to do so can cause greater harm to them and us. So learning to know the difference between what you can change and what you can't is a vital step towards recovery. Following recognition, important steps are available for dealing with the stress or trauma that may have played a part in the progression of the illness.

There was a reason I chose Darwinism to compare Jungian theory to, and that is the importance of biology. For although Jung, to his credit, advised Roland Hazard that the illness could not be cured by medication. Jung, as far as I know, did not add that our biological processes can be given a better chance to cope with the effects of alcoholism and aid as an avoidance tool against the mind's addictive tendency to create reasons for relapse.

This goes back to what I previously stated about stopping, or at least reducing, sugar intake and poor quality foods that provide initial energy through an increase in blood sugar levels, but then quickly lower your energy reserves shortly afterwards.

This is dangerous to an alcoholic, as is caffeine and other addictive substances as it makes them especially vulnerable. A caffeine hangover can be all it takes for you to falter and accept an alcoholic drink.

Likewise, smoking affects your nervous system, and as it goes hand in hand with alcohol, one can remind the brain of the other. Saying all that, if you are really far gone in alcoholism, too much change at once is too big an effort and sometimes, psychologically, you require something to rely on, at least to start with anyway.

Then, as abstinence becomes slightly easier, it should be remembered to avoid smoking, caffeine, refined sugar, white flour and other nutrient-lacking foods and fluids.

AA makes regular reference to God in the twelve steps, although it can be found in their literature that there are as many religious and non-religious beliefs and other interpretations, as there are members. The twelfth step states: 'having had a spiritual awakening as the result of these steps, we tried to carry this message to alcoholics, and to practise these principles in all our affairs.' AA goes on to explain that 'you need only to come to believe that a power greater than yourself exits and is much more capable than running your daily life than you have shown yourself to be, for some that power is the AA group, or the Fellowship as a whole'.

For me personally it is *Being*, one all-encompassing God, the Creator, the God of all Gods. I am not religious these days, having found truths and questionable beliefs in many religions, but above all, the misconception of these various beliefs by the people who practise them has pushed me away from religion. I am however, a believer in a higher power and I do not think that it is important what you name it, as long as you have the humility to believe that some force or power exists, greater than ourselves.

For me, the closest explanations for the unknown, that respect other religious beliefs by accepting that much of their essential beliefs are true, come from the eastern philosophical religions Hinduism and Buddhism. For me, their systems capture the personal experiences that I went through.

For other people the truth may be found in science or atheism. An atheist can often have spiritual beliefs of a higher power, be it mother nature, continuation of the human soul, past life beliefs, etc. A Scientist will believe what is proven to be correct through objective observation and measurement. So that is where my focus now resides, in the *Science of Being*.

Part of the AA programme consists of creating a moral inventory that has a use to the writer of being able to start forgiveness of oneself. To make amends to those whom you have hurt by your actions.

Obviously, those you apologise to, may not forgive you, but recognition is such a good start. Forgiveness will follow, even if it is just a nudge toward self forgiveness, to begin with.

"An alcoholic is a person for whom one drink is too many, and a hundred are not enough", AA handout literature.

38 YOGA & THE MEANING OF LIFE

To avoid confusing you, I'll just let you know that I've jumped about a year or two into the future now and to save you any boring details we're now at stage of my life where I have a partner and she is pregnant with my first child. During my girlfriend's pregnancy we attended regular weekly Yoga sessions, held in a beautiful location, in an old private school grounds. The newly refurbished hall had a fantastic view of the rolling, east-facing hills.

The Yoga teacher would sit with her back to the window, the glass covered almost the entire width and height of the wall. In the late summer/autumn evenings this west-facing room was perfectly positioned for viewing the most amazing sunsets over the beautiful Scottish hillside.

These few months of weekly Yoga practise gave me the foundation for a daily workout each morning. From remembering my favourite poses I then later came across the Rising Sun sequence. This was also described as the Sun Worship pose, as illustrated in a monthly Yoga magazine.

The daily yoga, including some Chi Gong exercises, kept my muscle tension in check, around the neck and shoulder areas where I was, like most people, susceptible to holding a lot of tension caused by everyday stress, driving and just general aches from sleeping and getting older.

These daily exercises would take from two to ten minutes, depending on how many cycles I did, which was dependent upon how much time I had spare, usually not a lot. If I had enough time to meditate, thirty minutes all-in including preparations, then I would do that instead, as meditating eases all muscle tension and gets the life-force flowing better than any Yoga Asana can.

When my first beautiful child was born it was a *peak experience*, her eyes were so alert and she looked to be full of awareness, of consciousness itself. The feeling of love from the moment she was born was so intense, it made me realise why people also say life is about love. I believe that this is true also, love is a word that cannot convey the real meaning, like most words that describe consciousness or being. Yoga means union, of all things, of mind, body, God and everything in and around us. Love is the realisation of this.

To truly love someone or something is to be in unison with that particular thing, to be such a defining part of it, such as father and child, that the two may almost be whole.

This is how I felt becoming a father, that my daughter was dependent upon me and to some extent I became dependent upon her; similar to the relationship with my wife, where we naturally helped each other be whole through our opposite personalities.

My natural fight against addiction was hugely fought from the feeling of love created from being a father. Also, the duties and responsibilities of being a father distract the mind from the need to seek other forms of happiness. The love and challenges created within a new family can either make you or brake you, fortunately for me, they made me.

I am not alone in my belief that there is a deeper learning in life than in university, the psychologist Abraham Maslow changed his whole psychology outlook following the birth of his second child and claims to have learnt much more from his marriage and his children being born. He also highly rates psychoanalysis of self, which in terms of Yoga is meditating and later analysing the process of thought.

Space is made between thinking to understand what thought becomes. A thought bubbles up from being into our consciousness.

First of all the subtle thought appears on our subconscious mind and creates feelings. These feelings give rise to and become energy, in motion (emotion) and this is how actions including re-actions, are carried out.

You don't have to study psychology to appreciate this. Self-analysis is available to everyone and in my opinion should be done before setting out to interact in a dependable way with other human beings. You owe it to yourself to know yourself, you owe other people the respect of being independently observed and experienced without your pre-judging analysis, based on aspects of your own self-awareness or lack of it.

There are schools now around the world, set up through the Transcendental Meditation programme, that include this internal learning as well as the normal associative learning. From learning about yourself first and continuing to do so as you progress through your education, a holistic learning of the usual external subjects is made possible.

Self actualisation is the top of Maslow's pyramid, or hierarchy, of needs. It represents the incorporation of your Self, your Being, into all of your external experiences. The two become so integrated that the person enjoying self actualisation witnesses the beauty of creation in all things and understands his fellow human beings, respecting them for all of their perfections and imperfections.

University was going well, my grades were good and I could afford to slip a little and still pass. I was worried that slippage would be inevitable when our new baby was born. It turned out okay though, due to my worrying I studied harder and somehow managed to obtain a first class honours.

Our second beautiful creation caused another peak experience. I'll never forget both experiences, whilst I have my mind intact, for as long as I live. My girls have made my life worth living and working hard for, everything I did was to give them a better quality of life. Sleep deprivation was a problem though, it turned out that both of our girls had sleep apnoea and they had to have their tonsils removed. Once they did life got easier, but at this stage it was only our eldest who had had the operation.

Our youngest had to reach a weight of fifteen kilograms before it was deemed safe for her to undergo the operation, due to the risk of blood loss compared to the amount of blood she had, so for my whole degree it was nights on the couch with her resting on my chest and me reading a book. I probably have them to thank for my good grades. I was now working back in construction as Site Engineer and studying a degree part time, one day a week.

Yoga meditation was infrequent, but I did do it whenever I wasn't so tired I fell asleep in the midst of it, which was often the case. Before exams I would make an extra effort because the twenty minutes time out would allow a productive study day and prevent me from stressing out and getting nervous. Sometimes transcendence towards the end of the twenty minutes would occur, as this is how the mindfulness of breathing technique works, it usually takes the first fifteen minutes or so to still the mind.

39 CONSCIOUS CYCLES

When I started on the construction of Crieff High School in 2008, I had just recently decided to abstain again from alcohol. I managed nearly three years exactly without AA meetings, but I followed the twelve steps as best I could, kept a journal of my addictive, automatic urges and avoided drinking situations; therefore remaining aware of my addiction.

These three years passed very quickly due to the continual studying and management of the construction of the high school. Pressure was intense, if I had taken a drink it would have been fatal for me, I would have crashed and risked losing everything.

My time at university and the high school construction ran together and ended around the same time. The term 'conscious cycles' came to me years before, whilst I was working at Loch Katrine, hiring bikes, and I remember my mate, who became a best friend, saying, 'more like unconscious cycles'. Which was funny because at that time we were more unconscious of the cycles of life, from still dabbling in cannabis and alcohol and the occasional episode of ecstasy.

You would think, after my spiritual experience and fear of psychosis, that I would have completely avoided that lifestyle, but it is difficult to change habits of a lifetime. Hence the reason many revisit hospital time and time again.

I was determined even then not to go back to the way I had been. Fortunately, the one-offs didn't put me back there, although I remember some close-shaves, usually the following morning when feeling fragile, or lying in bed trying to go to sleep. It was a battle to hold on sometimes.

Back to the future. This era, whilst I was at uni and constructing the school was probably where I truly began to become conscious of my mind's desires and cycles of thought, including an awareness of addictive impulses. It was a mixture, I believe, of meditation, although irregular, and abstinence from alcohol.

From this foundation, a meeting of similar, like-minded people continued to help me stay on track, naturally, without trying to help. This is the best kind of healing, I believe. For example, my first day at university, a few months before I commenced total abstinence, I sat next to a guy from Libya. He lived in Edinburgh, had a daughter around the same age as mine and being Arabic he didn't drink alcohol either.

Like me he was a part-time student and we hit it off well. I cannot remember having a non-drinking friend before this. I think this might be one of the reasons AA works so well. They advise us to associate with non-drinkers as much as possible.

40 REAL LIFE RISK ASSESSMENT

Following completion of university and my youngest daughter's operation to remove her tonsils to cure her sleep apnoea, life began to get a little easier. With this ease however, returned the dangers of alcoholism. You would think that the stress of studying for exams, having little sleep and a stressful job would have caused a greater need for wanting a drink.

It was in fact the lack of desperation to succeed and the reality that having studied so hard to obtain a degree, I was nowhere nearer to a higher quality of life than before I started. My wife was fed-up from always worrying about money and not having had a holiday since before we got together. Life for us was work, work, work, but despite this we were a happy family and our daughters were very happy.

We had a little money saved and were hoping to move house upon finishing upgrading our own home, but the realisation of not having enough income to afford a bigger mortgage, made us decide to spend the little amount we had saved, on the holiday of a lifetime. We took our four and one-year-old daughters to Disneyworld, Florida. It was a memorable holiday. On return things went back to normal of course, except my wife had obtained a work placement earlier in the year through a course she attended that focused on getting professional people back into work. The prolonged recession was making it very difficult to find work and people in jobs valued them and were not likely to be getting any salary rises soon.

The work placement was a success, although no opportunities were directly available after the placement. She was obviously highly thought of because a position did become available later in the year. It was a temporary role to begin with and this turned into a permanent job after about six months.

Before the permanent position became available life was still up in the air. Struggling to find a way to accomplish a better standard of living, I took an interest in the stock market. A mate at work introduced me to watching stocks on the internet and I bought my first trade shortly afterwards. I made the mistake of buying this first trade on the downward trend of the share price and solely focused on the current price in relative terms to it's fifty two week high and low prices. I then failed to wait until the price rose back up and decided to cut my losses, which amounted to only a few pounds.

At least a year passed by, before I placed my next trade. I had developed a basic spreadsheet to keep a record of shares bought, trading fees and stamp duty. I had also read a little more about valuing companies and not just picking shares based on their current market value. This was a good distraction from the boredom of work, it probably was also another potential addiction arising and potentially the negative emotion of greed creeping in. However, what I remember as my main driver was my conscious need to feel like I was giving my family the best life possible. It didn't seem to be happening quickly enough, work was busy, but promotion was non existent and the recession was still holding on with all it's might. It turned out to be the longest global recession since World War two.

Life was a little less than expected and awareness of this from my wife's perspective was only too real. Until she got the permanent new job. Being made permanent staff came with travel opportunities and within six months she had travelled to China, Israel, and various places in Europe. From a distraction of swapping addictive lifestyles from drinking to studying and then to researching share trading, I was still sober, until just before my third year anniversary of commencing total abstinence.

It was Christmas time and my wife had decided that she would have a drink at her Christmas party, despite having been off it entirely for longer than me. She just didn't like getting drunk apparently, although it might have commenced from being pregnant, then having witnessed my problems, plus not appealing as much, to the negative hung-over feelings that followed. I really believed she wasn't interested in drinking again.

This was a test for me, not set intentionally by my wife, just a coincidence, yet a test all the same. The TV adverts had already been taunting me for a couple of weeks on the lead up to Christmas, as they did every year. If it wasn't for my daughter's loving Christmas, I would hate it, I really would. As it happens they made it really magical and despite the temptation of consuming alcohol, I love the Christmas holidays. One night an advert on some alcoholic drink ends, and I burst into tears on the couch next to my wife. I confide in her and tell her that despite looking strong, three years have passed and yet my brain still has a mind of it's own to desire alcohol and I admit that I do not know if it will ever stop. I think she may have offered not to go out on her Christmas night out, but knowing that she would resent me for it, I told her not to be so silly and to go.

After her Christmas party I was in the local hotel, buying a new friend in the village a pint after he helped us fit a kitchen for a very cheap price. Maybe because he didn't know I was a non-drinker, I bought myself a shandy and broke the abstinence. I had 4 pints that night and forgot I had a problem. I then told my wife the next day that I had taken a few shandys and felt fine and that I was cured. I told her that I thought I could handle the occasional few drinks and keep it under control. To some extent I really believed this, although shrouded with deep doubts. Obviously she was very surprised, following my recent tearful admission and she voiced her concerns, but at the same time she understood the equally hard task of being completely abstinent.

You see, for an alcoholic, one drink is too much and a hundred is not enough. It would only be a matter of time before addiction kicked in and the alcohol took over my limited control. Yet a full year and a half went by of irregular social drinking, no black-outs or actions of regret. I was actually beginning to think that just possibly I had this cracked. I was living a normal life, not feeling so much the social outsider anymore.

Then a real life risk assessment had to be made when some changing factors to my personal life unravelled. This came about after a few months of plain sailing. The idea of plain sailing is a welcome one for an addict, for a change not having to protect oneself from encounters and reactive thinking that may lead to a relapse. Generally this is a common phenomena of progressive alcohol and drug addiction taking life for granted and forgetting the chaos that eventually follows a slow regression back to powerlessness.

We had finally completed upgrading our house and garden and had sold our home. The moving out date was at the end of the Christmas holidays and I was living away again in the north of Scotland, upgrading a sewage treatment works. My wife had endured two previous summers of being a working Mum and lone parent during the week, because the recession had taken me down to England, working.

I was applying for jobs locally and although the construction sector was still suffering, there were some definite signs of recovery.

It turned out that the company beginning to win most of the work in Scotland was the one I currently worked for, and most recruiters advised me to stay put, the trust-worthy ones anyway, who had long term relationships in mind and not instant commissions. You see, it is a small world and any recruitment agent worth their salt knows that playing the long-term game is more rewarding.

The person they fix up in a new role may one day become the hirer of future employees.

Eventually from continued working away from home, my relationship broke down beyond repair. My world shattered around me.

41 CUTTING OUT THE CAFFEINE

No controls were laid out for the scenario I found myself in now, for my life-risk assessment didn't include this.

Then my old, darker self, lurking in the background, waiting for his chance to reappear, came back into my life, offering short-term happiness and a place to forget my feelings of despair. Alcohol consumption stepped up from the occasional social swallie to a regular weekly intake. Fortunately the company I shared whilst working away from home was mature and not alcoholics, so an element of control was kept in check, yet how is a mystery to me even now. Once an alcoholic admits he has a problem, to himself at least, there is no turning back, it is impossible to remain in denial, unless you suffer from other forms of mental instability.

Having spent too many mornings suffering from mild hangovers and feelings of worthlessness and despair, another ploy to be free of this disease once and for all, emerged into my consciousness. I had been getting depressed, and was acting really manic at work, when I was busy, tired or overly stressed; so I picked myself up in a small way and began little steps to reduce my desire to drink alcohol. It started with trying to reduce my caffeine intake.

It may sound silly, but when you are used to a heavy intake of intoxicants you don't experience the more subtle sensations of coffee, it is however, a strong stimulant, that can be experienced in its full power when the body is first cleansed of all other stimulants, and intoxicants. It is also worth noting that coffee, in excess of a moderate daily intake, is highly dangerous for an alcoholic or other drug abuser. Once the body gets used to the sensation, it sends signals to the mind for more stimulus and as the coffee becomes less effective, the mind seeks other remedies; and all of this goes on in an area of the subconscious that we have no conscious control over.

Although the source of our habits maybe deeply rooted, the delicate experience of desires changing form can be realised on the conscious level. This is a tool for experiencing how the body/mind relationship works and can be a key to unlocking the insanity of auto-responsive thinking. This may further, through practise of contemplation, which is greatly helped by meditation and mindfulness of our actions, provide the beginnings of gaining control of our thoughts. Of course, you could eliminate the danger by not drinking coffee at all, and if you don't already, and have an addictive nature, then best not to start in the first place.

42 BACK TO THE FUTURE

This was very nearly re-named 'relapse 2', following the end of true love, it seems. Although this isn't necessarily true, for I will always love the one who gave me two delightful daughters and true friends for life; so true love remains, only 'in love' ends.

Love is a difficult word to understand. At this juncture of my life, physical, tangible love has simplified to fatherly love, for my wife as well as my children. Having learnt that my wife no longer loves me as a partner, more as a father and friend, my magnetic poles reversed. I am upside down and inside out. Oh it would be so easy to give in and go back to the old Steve-O, but no, I take responsibility for my actions now. I have two amazing daughters to care for and of course, self respect and respect for everything that has caused me to be and helped me regain myself.

To fail myself would be to let down those who have helped me so many times. Lots of people can love you but there is no doubt who, when those who have seen you at your worst and continue to love you still.

Now I will not disillusion you and pretend I was almighty, strong and perfect. It is deeply set in my character to seek substance that will relieve my immediate suffering.

If meditation does not help quickly enough, self medication can. However, the recovery is more painful this way and longer, as alcohol has a depressive and desensitising effect, making it harder to reach a state of peace and calmness. The after-effects are pure chaos in motion, lack of control and ability to function on a normal level. Oh yes, people do notice.

For a short while I even thought of booking myself back into hospital, it wouldn't have taken much to fake a psychosis, in fact some mornings I wasn't far away from losing track of reality. I wasn't drinking large amounts, it was just the state of mind I was in and the fact that my body and mind, like most alcoholics is allergic to the stuff.

From just a little, my side ached and my skin became blotchy red, probably age catching up with me, but liver spots started to show on my nose and cheeks.

Thirty-four-years-old and age was starting to creep up faster in four months than it had in four years. Frequently, I asked myself, 'what was happening inside of my body and what was I doing to my mind?'

It is time to take action.

What have I really wanted to do but not been able to, due to money and feeling guilty of spending so much on myself? No, not a sailing boat or a holiday. I remembered that I had wanted to learn Transcendental Meditation, and I figured that it might be my ticket to safety and freedom, and hopefully peaceful happiness.

It's possibly a pity that it takes tough negative emotional experiences to kick us into doing something good for ourselves, but I'm not complaining, at least I had that chance and knowledge that something might be out there to help me through the dark times. This is the biggest reason I share this story, there is no greater gift I could give someone than passing on the positive attributes of meditation.

This leads me on to explain that although mindfulness pulled me out of the woods long enough for me to meet a partner who helped me in opposite ways, it is not quite as deep or instantaneous as Transcendental (deep) Meditation (TM). Having decided that this was what I ought to do, to learn Transcendental Meditation, a change took place within me for the better.

In preparation for the daily commitment of twenty-minute sessions, twice a day, to meditate, I returned to the mindfulness technique on a daily basis and during the summer months I managed to find the time.

These windows of opportunity, in a usually very busy day, opened up and included tranquil river settings where I took twenty minutes to sit cross-legged on a large rock under a thick canopy of trees. No one ever disturbed me as it was off the path and unseen to passers-by.

The meditation gave me a renewed awareness and drive for success. It gave me the foresight to avoid potential drinking scenarios and the alcohol consumption started to get back in check, although slowly and not wholeheartedly.

43 TRANSCENDENTAL DEEP MEDITATION

Mindfulness is still exactly that, mindful; although of the subtlest sense, touch. The feeling of breath entering and exiting the body at the subtlest point, the end of our nose, and transcending this subtle experience, whilst the mind is still. It does work. It is as good as TM once you finally get to transcend, and there is no reason to change your practise if it suits you, it's just that TM is so much easier and direct to the source of Consciousness.

I did find it a little strange swapping mindfulness to TM because of the renewed daily practise of mindfulness of breathing. I say daily but I did miss some, and because I had struggled to keep up a daily practise of mindfulness prior to starting TM I was worried that I would pay a lot of money to learn and not be able to keep it up. Subsequently I was surprised on two accounts, one was the ease of reaching a meditative state, not fifteen to twenty minutes in, but at anytime into it. Instantaneous was definitely the word to describe it.

The second surprise was the ease of finding time to do it. I think, because it is so instantaneous and effective, our mind is given a little insight into the nature of pure consciousness or being, at an early enough stage in the practise for it to realise that real happiness is nearer than we realised.

The nature of the mind is to seek happiness, hence the reason we continually do what we do: eat chocolate, partake in thrill-seeking and risky sport, or whatever people do that they enjoy, we seek happiness all of our lives.

Unfortunately, the happiness we find on the relative level of experience is usually better in the first experience of it and then gradually fades the more we re-visit or carry out the action that brought such happiness the first time.

Although I cannot describe the teachings of what I learnt, I can say that I have experienced real fulfilment and happiness since learning and it doesn't fade or become toxic like some relative experiences can after excess.

Did I automatically stop drinking and regain an instantaneous remedy for my emotionally unstable mindset?

No. I did, however, begin to water the root, and it takes some time to enjoy the fruit. After about three months in, I began to feel some structure appearing and some meaningful points were becoming visible to me in terms of what I was going through in my everyday experiences.

Karma, or action, eternal in its nature was still pulling me here and there; but I was becoming aware of it and through awareness, was almost able to understand why, and at least not let the external influences of life continue to affect me so much.

I was in a storm and it raged all around me. It also rarely let up for at least a year, and when it did I wasn't sure it was safe to breathe a sigh of relief for fear it would start again and pull me under. There is always a positive to a negative and always the same strength. So when in the thick of it try and remember that in these times we are more likely to experience a peak experience

Likewise remember, when the going gets tough, the tough get going, and when the going gets good, we should be on standby and alert. When you think everything is great this is usually a good time to remain alert.

'Why?' I hear you ask!

When we are feeling up, a down may follow, and when feeling down an up will follow, we don't have to be bi-polar to understand this, nor will the normal mind be free of it. A middle road of sustained happiness is possible. I suggested just a short time ago, that karma, or action, can be witnessed whilst in the midst of action.

This is not a mental technique, to try it mentally would be to break your mind in two and the result most likely would involve a stretch in the local mental hospital.

Let us rest our minds and attention and learn a little about the giver of such supreme knowledge, the great Yoga Master himself, the man who brought Transcendental Deep Meditation to the Western world, Maharishi Mahesh Yogi.

"The basic fundamental of behavior should be to give. When you are going to meet someone, think what you are going to give him, whether it be a concrete gift of a beautiful object, words of greeting, warm sympathy, praise, adoration, love, elevating advice, or good news for his body, mind or soul. . . The art of behavior is such that the first moment of the meeting should have a real value of the meeting of the two hearts."

Maharishi Mahesh Yogi: Science of Being and Art of Living, p180

He has stated so much wisdom, expressing his thoughts, that explain infinite wisdom in so little dialogue. If ever there was proof in our modern age of someone acting from Being, he was it.

'Skill in action', he called it.

Where the action is at maximum force, with the least amount of effort. This is because the activity of the mind of the doer, is first reduced to nil, none active, pure potential, and from this point his actions are from the truest part of himself. From cosmic consciousness thoughts arise and maintain innocence, they do not become diluted with other thoughts and so attain the highest results with the least amount of effort, for they are favoured by the cosmos. A factor of this phenomenon includes freedom from the binding of action, or karma, for the doer.

This freedom is again what I was referring to previously. It comes naturally as a result of prolonged meditation. It cannot be mentally practised or achieved through any manner of mental intention.

The practise of TM can be referred to as a mental technique, however if practised the experience proves that it is so much more than that.

Transcendence is what occurs when the mental repetition of a proper thought is practised. This technique, TM, must be given by an experienced teacher, for a number of reasons.

The most important being the choice of thought, there are a limited number of pure thoughts, designed to assist in transcendence and having no meaning. The teachers are trained how to assign a mantra to an individual. These selection factors are unknown to non-teachers. There is another important reason that TM is not self-taught from a book. That is, having a guide, to check your meditation and assess your development through your continued experiences and questions that may arise.

TM is a life long journey for the dedicated, with many benefits along the way. Back in 1963 Maharish published his book, *The Science of Being and Art of Living*, and he described how physical science will develop into the science of mental phenomena. I believe we are very close to that now.

Maharishi discussed Einstein's theory of relativity, recognising how it is correct that everything in the universe can only be understood relatively. However Einstein also sought to derive a Unified Field Theory, on the basis that there must be one common denominator for all of creation.

This one element of basic unity of all material existence is described by Maharishi as Being. Maharishi describes the field of the Being as ranging from an absolute, un-manifested, eternal state to the relative, active and forever changing states.

"The Being is eternally never-changing in its absolute state, and it is eternally ever-changing in its relative states."

Maharishi Mahesh Yogi. The Science of Being and Art of Living, p31.

Maharishi often explained this usually unfathomable knowledge using analogies. One such helpful aid, is considering the properties of gas, water and ice. They each vary in their properties, but the essential content is the same: oxygen and hydrogen atoms.

"As the oxygen and hydrogen remaining in their never-changing states are found exhibiting different qualities, so also the Being, remaining in its never-changing, eternal absolute character, is found expressing itself in the different forms and phenomena of the diverse creation."

Maharishi. The Science of Being and Art of Living, p31

TM is the technique used to transcend the manifest relative state of Being to experience the absolute state of Being, and in doing so, gain the benefits of this infinite reservoir of energy and awareness.

Transcendence is possible via practising subtler experiences of any object, through any of the senses, until its finest state is realised. On transcending that finest state, one will arrive at the state of absolute Being. TM is an effortless technique that uses thought, hinted by Maharishi to be because of its vibration.

Maharishi explained how thinking is the subtle state of speech and speech is sound. It is said in Ancient Indian philosophy that the universe and all of creation is based on vibration. Particle physics is proving the same, that the finite elements are not stable as once thought.

44 RIGHT THINKING, LEFT FEELING

Having drawn back the bow in meditation and letting the arrow hit it's target naturally and effortlessly, self realisation via conscious thinking equates to thinking well and feeling well. It is a wholeness that is worth seeking, and keeping once finding, although life's pressures can get in the way of maintaining a healthy outlook all of the time.

The following may arguably be deemed too much right-brain-sided thinking and not necessarily positive thought in action, and may result in feelings of anxiety. Still, if the mind is grounded from regular relaxation and there are no conscious insecurities then I believe it is perfectly safe to explore some depths. It was during such a personal exploration that I came up with the following.

Contemplation of oneness popped up again from an infrequent set of experiences via the radio, during a lone car journey across Scotland's highlands. Even though the personal experiences of oneness are relatively rare, they often occur frequently enough to be owed some respectful insightfulness, and so, two of my better theories unfold.

THE UNIVERSITY OF LIFE; A JOURNEY OF THE MIND

<u>First theory:</u>

Oneness might occur because the subconscious is aware of the early stages of thought and because we are all connected and the thoughts come from the same source. The subconscious mind is aware of these subtle thoughts arriving before they reach our everyday waking consciousness.

If these faint initial thoughts are extremely fast, beyond what we are used to experiencing, it could be possible that it seems like the thoughts are arriving at the same time, as a coincidence, and as you experience the oneness. Therefore, the (subconscious) mind may have already been aware of the forthcoming event (e.g. a specific word about to be broadcast on the radio, or a road sign about to come into sight) which prompted a similar thought, but a different one nevertheless, during a multi light-speed process that we can't consciously comprehend.

You may ask: what would be the reason for all of this? Well there may be none sometimes, maybe other times it is a signal from your subconscious to your waking-state consciousness to take heed of something. It may be telling you to relax, like today, driving home from a skiing trip I was fretting about personal issues regarding my marriage breakdown, and a sign caught my eye at the precise moment I was thinking I need to be free of these worries.

The sign was *Freedom*. It was in respect to something about Scotland, but it was the main word that caught my attention. Another experience in the same journey, was through radio one(ness), it was actually the channel radio 1. The presenter this time said a whole sentence where the first four words exactly matched the thoughts in my head, at precisely the same time! There had been no discussions related to the topic of the sentence as they were referring to different call-ins from various people. The message was:

'…for people opening cafes today… blah, blah, blah.'

My thought on cue of *'for'* was about opening my own cafe one day!

When you know that you are thinking clearly, not manically, and in as normal a state of mind as you ever could be, and these coincidences continually occur, it would be crazy not to consider the possibilities. If all the coincidences were meaningless, as I keep telling myself they are, then it may not be worth looking into. However, I cannot deny the high frequency of these symbolic events. Edging on caution at least, I will admit that this is a route to psychosis and manic behaviour. I think due to over conscious thinking of something too far beyond normal conscious awareness is just a sure way to brake your conscious mind and give yourself a major headache.

This theory then rests on the idea of the source of thought being the same source for the live radio presenter as the subject (e.g. me) and the subject's subconsciousness being receptive to the radio presenter's finer thoughts, before those thoughts reach the presenter's consciousness. To provide a coincidental situation, in this case, a similar thought via voice.

There are two possible problems or complications to this theory:

1) Recording, how does the mind pick up reception to this if the recording was made prior to the coincidental occurrence?

2) The connection between the presenter and the subject receiving, how can this be possible at even the subatomic level; how would the subconscious mind be able to pick out another being's thoughts, especially a particular person, hundreds of miles away in a city with 13.6 million others around it.

Problem one could be tested, through journals of experiences and noting if they were from live, or recorded broadcasters; and what about visuals, like the sign for example?

Second theory:

My second theory of this phenomena, that might even be classed as a form of psychic phenomena is as follows. Supposing that a thought has no physical mass then it might be possible, based on Einstein's theory of relativity, for time travel of our sub consciousness to take place. Sounds crazy I know, but if we consider the mechanics of travelling at the speed of light, then it can be seen that this, in theory, is possible.

I do not claim to understand particle physics, although I think that it may become an interest of mine to learn more about it, as it seems that it is this area of science that is pushing the boundaries closer to understanding what consciousness is. My great uncle Frank, whom I've made reference to throughout this book, collated a lifetimes worth of references to the light. The Anthology of Light, is his so far unpublished works, which is a list of extracts from a wide range of material on the references to both the inner and outer light, but mostly inner.

From reading Frank's Anthology of Light, I came across an interesting extract: From Science to God: Peter Russell (New World Library)

For an observer actually travelling at the speed of light, the equations of special relativity predict that time would come to a complete standstill, and length would shrink to nothing. Physicists usually avoid considering this strange state of affairs by saying nothing can ever attain the speed of light, so we don't have to worry about any bizarre things that might occur at that speed.

When physicists say nothing can ever attain the speed of light, they are referring to objects with mass. Einstein showed that not only do space and time change as speed increases, so does mass. In the case of mass, however, the change is an increase rather than a decrease; the faster something moves, the greater it's mass becomes. If an object were to ever reach the speed of light its mass would become infinite.

Light, having no mass, can travel at the speed of light. If you could travel at speeds near to the speed of light, time and space would change according to your speed. As you get faster, time slows down and distance appears to be less, i.e. space becomes compressed.

'Nor is it just time that changes; space is also affected. As an observer approaches the speed of light, measurements of length (that is, measurements of space in the direction of motion) get shorter, and in exactly the same proportion as time slows. If you were passing by me at 80 percent the speed of light, lengths in your universe would have shrunk to one-third of mine.'

From Science to God: Peter Russell (New World Library)

Scientific experiments have been carried out to verify these affects, including atomic clocks being flown at very high velocities and observations of time recorded to be slower. Further, subatomic particles have been flown at speeds close to the speed of light and quite recently, on the 4th July 2012, the discovery of the Higgs Boson (the God) particle was made.

'The idea of a field that fills the entire universe, mediated with a particle of zero spin, with a non-determined mass, a so-called scalar boson, giving mass to other particles, is definitely a counterintuitive one and certainly very different'.

World Science Festival,

http://worldsciencefestival.com/events/higgs_boson_announcement

In basic terms this finding creates a new platform for Scientists to develop new physics and further understand the common-sense-denying subject of quantum mechanics; including the realities of time and space when travelling at the speed of light.

Having considered the above and assuming that there is a fourth state of consciousness, termed 'pure consciousness', then it might be possible for our sub consciousness to be able to pick up future events before they occur, and that these thoughts might be recognised intuitively.

Time travel of a thing with no mass may now be realised with Einstein's theory of relativity. So if thoughts, like light, have no mass; then it might be possible to grasp the outline of how our thoughts arise from pure consciousness.

If pure consciousness is all encompassing and everywhere at once due to it's nature, best described as Light, it's reality if it could experience one, would be that time has appeared to have stopped, or that there is no time and that there is no space either, because space is compressed; hence why consciousness is said to infuse everything and be everywhere.

This being said, it can now be considered that thoughts appear on our consciousness from pure consciousness (the source of thought and all things).

Therefore if in the process of the thoughts appearing in our mind, as random as they do, our conscious mind becomes aware of it, however subtly; then this can be a very rough explanation for experiencing Oneness.

To clarify the theory, the future voice on the radio or sighting of a sign around the corner, can be occasionally observed, because our thoughts come from an area of ourselves that is not bound by the relativity of time and space, where time slows as space (length) shortens and mass increases.

I believe that this is why the Self (Pure Consciousness) is described as being unbounded and infinite and another example that backs up the above theory, is one from a Yogi who has written down a record of his experiences.

45 PEACE & TRANQUIL-I-TEA

Well, we've come full circle. Ten years in the making, from a period of self-reflection after leaving the psychiatric hospital, with new beginnings and new opportunities. Having shown you that even the most unlikely candidate for going to university can, in fact, obtain a higher education and a good one at that may provide some hope, if that's what you desire.

However, nothing beats the University of Life and I am grateful for all of the experiences in my life, even the negative ones. Possibly more so the negative ones, for they were like the Tamas destructive predominance that enabled the Sattvic creation of a new activity born of Rajas; and so the Three Gunas, in their varying forms manipulated my life in order for the wood to be cut from the trees.

They freed me of dragging debris, so my vessel of continuously flowing, eternal life-force, moved more swiftly through the ocean of life, with less drag and more momentum toward a more fulfilling existence.

Wisdom is not just pain it is a chance for a better life, to be a better person. I do not profess to actually be a better person, nor to be wise, just possibly be a little more thoughtful. For who can truly foresee the reaction to all of his or her actions, no matter how mindful they are?

The truth is that ten years on from commencing this story, where the final chapter was tentatively titled Peace & Tranquil-I-tea, in a vain hope for some miraculous spiritual enlightenment, where just drinking a nice herbal tea might assist me on my merry way. A fact of life is, anything can happen at any moment, to the best and to the worst. Bad things happen to innocent people, accidents happen, disasters occur; it is how we can pick ourselves up afterwards and still remain grateful for life that matters.

Pockets of real peace can be found in the most un-peaceful situations. Bliss happiness and peak experiences can be found in the most despairing situations. Life is a mystery and that's what makes it worth living. I hope that you have enjoyed my journey and are not too disappointed that it appears to have brought you back to the beginning.

It wasn't meant to end this way, but ironically, it does reflect the cycle of life and this is The University of Life. All things in life can be found to be within a cycle, it doesn't matter what aspect you consider, things are created then destroyed and something occurs in between. Hence the Three Gunas will surely be further investigated in western science in the years to come and likely some scientific experiments shall provide a better understanding and a platform for a higher aspiration of human evolution, than exists currently.

For those with addictive personalities or similarly struggling with loved one's problems, the truth is: addiction once realised, is never beat; for if it has been realised, it means that it has already become rooted in the person's psyche. Fear not though, for it can be tamed and controlled.

Life can be enjoyed with little effort, of regular gentle reminders of how bad things can get if you don't stay on the path and avoidance of the foods and liquids that give the addictions energy.

This includes all addictions, not just mind-altering from drugs and alcohol, but too much sex, gambling, etc. Meditation and further understanding of the inherent experiences coming in and out of meditation, through some of the references within this book, should protect us from further plunges into the abyss.

A blog will remain open at https://www.facebook.com/SRPCosmos/ for anyone who feels that they need to discuss any of the detail within this book, or anything that happens afterwards, from reading it.

I would like to end on the following quote and thank you for sticking with me on this journey to potential freedom. For whatever happens next in my life, I feel that I am at least on a good foundation of understanding, with no regrets, remorse or negative feelings towards anyone in my life. That must be a good start to an end and I wish the same for you and all of your loved ones.

'All fear death at some point, however not to succumb to despair, an artist's job should be to find an antidote for existence'.

Unknown quoter. Possibly Friedrich Nietzsche.

ABOUT THE AUTHOR

Steven is an Incorporated Member of the Institute of Civil Engineers. Having gained a first class BSc Honours degree in civil engineering, Steven uses his interest of Science and philosophy to present philosophical ideas in a way that everyday readers can relate to. Having had an awakening in 2004, he sought to help others through an idea of a University for All. Being a Transcendental Meditator and Sidha, he is on a journey of inner peace and discovery of creation.

Printed in Great Britain
by Amazon